# contents

# introduction

There is something special about giving a handmade gift. The birth of a baby, that memorable first day at school, holidays, birthdays or "just because I was thinking about you" are all perfect occasions for making and giving.

My love of handmade presents arrived with the premature birth of my first son. Too small to fit into most other baby clothes, our prized possession was a small handmade hat from a friend. Looking back now, it was full of mistakes—she was just learning to crochet at the time—but he wore that hat daily until I could no longer pull it over his ears. It was as if he was carrying around a bit of love from his beloved godmother.

And therein, I think, lies the beauty of handmade gifts. It is not just about the finished object, but the love, care and thought that goes into the entire process—from picking out the yarn to sewing in the ends. It says to the recipient that they mean enough to us to give up our most precious resource for them—our time.

This book is filled with things to make for everyone in your life—from babies, to children, to friends, to men, to women and for all kinds of occasions. You may even find some things you would like to make for yourself.

Happy crocheting!
Kat
http://www.slugsontherefrigerator.com

# getting started

## yarns

Choosing yarn for gifts is really no different from choosing for yourself—think about how the recipient is going use and wear the item, how likely they will be to hand wash (or not) and buy the best you can afford.

Yarn has come a long way in recent years. An ever-expanding combination of weights and fibers is available with relative ease in your local wool shop or online yarn stores.

### Acrylic

There is no doubt that acrylic is the cheapest fiber available. Inexpensive, with many of the newer varieties being soft to the touch and machine washable, acrylic is a good option for giving. However, bear in mind that acrylic yarns often don't wear well and they can result in piled and misshapen items. They also have a tendency to "squeak" against the hook.

### Wool

You will see throughout the pages of this book that I show a strong preference for wool or wool blend yarns. Wool yarns, especially merino and Blue Faced Leicester, are a joy to work with. Most wool yarns available these days are soft enough to be worn against the skin. There are many machine washable wool yarns on the market—look for "superwash" on the label, particularly if you are giving your gift to someone who isn't a knitter or crocheter. It means your lovingly handmade present is more likely to be worn time and again by its recipient.

### Other Fibers

The fibers that can be spun into yarn are seemingly endless. Cotton and bamboo are great for items that need a lot of washing. Linen and jute are good choices for homewares that need structure. If you have questions about how a yarn will behave, ask a member of staff at your local store for advice.

### Substituting Yarn

In each pattern throughout the book, I have suggested a yarn that works well for the pattern in terms of weight, drape and washability. I have also given a few suggestions to help you find some other alternatives. In each pattern, I have also included the amount of yarn required, the yarn's properties and the weight. To ensure you are successful in substituting yarn, choose one with similar properties.

The easiest way to substitute yarn is to look for yarn of a similar make up. If the yarn called for is a 50/50 wool/alpaca mix, then start looking there. Of course you can substitute other materials, but if you are making something with a lot of drape, then make sure your yarn can do that for you.

### Yarn Weight Conversion

Yarn comes in a variety of different weights or thicknesses.

| USA weight | Australian/New Zealand weight |
|---|---|
| Lace | 2 ply |
| Light fingering | 3 ply |
| Fingering | 4 ply |
| Fingering (4ply) Sport (5ply) | 5 ply |
| DK (8ply) | 8 ply |
| Worsted/Aran | 10 ply |
| Bulky | 12 ply |
| Super bulky | 14 ply |

## hooks

Crochet hooks are predominately made out of wood, acrylic, aluminum or steel. Personally, I prefer the glide and feel of aluminum crochet hooks, as they are both affordable and work with most yarns. This is down to personal preference and it is worth trying out a few. I am guilty of only being able to use one particular brand of hooks for all of my crochet.

Crochet hooks are sized in relation to their diameter. A larger crochet hook will take more yarn into the stitch. Most of the time, larger hooks are used with heavier yarns and smaller hooks for finer weights.

## Tunisian Hooks

Tunisian, or Afghan, hooks are the same as traditional crochet hooks, but with a longer shaft or flexible cord attached with a stopper at the end. Tunisian hooks for working in the round have a hook at both ends, although in this book, Tunisian will only be worked in rows. Tunisian hooks can be bought separately or as part of a kit.

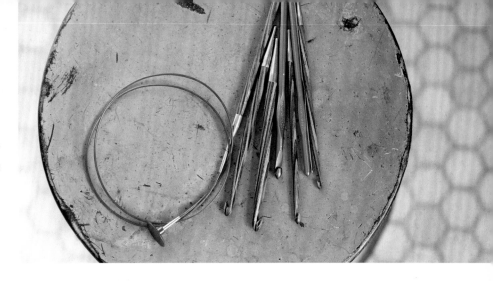

## other supplies

### Tapestry Needles

These have large eyes and blunt ends. They are used for sewing up or weaving in ends.

### Stitch Markers

Use the type that have a split ring or are open, as you will need to move them with each round or row. I often use just a scrap of yarn or a safety pin as a stitch marker, rather than buying anything special.

### Sewing Needles

Used particularly for sewing on buttons, these are thinner and sharper than tapestry needles. If you don't have co-ordinating thread for buttons, split your yarn lengthwise to thread through your sewing needle to sew on buttons.

### Scissors

Sharp embroidery scissors are particularly useful for crochet, allowing you to make precision cuts without a lot of bulk getting in the way or cutting your work.

### Buttons

Possibly my favorite part of making a garment is choosing the buttons. Remember, buttons can be choking hazards, so ensure they are sewn on very tightly and are checked regularly.

## sizing

For each pattern a sizing table indicates the key finished measurements. Each measurement has a guide for the age range the item will fit. Please remember that these are only guides. Where possible, use the actual measurements of the recipient to decide which size to make.

* Head Circumference: Measure around the head, just above the ears.
* Chest: Measure around the trunk, under the armpits.
* Bust: Measure the fullest part.
* Sleeve Length: Measure from the shoulder to the wrist.
* Length: Measure from the back of the neck to the waist.
* Waist: Measure around the natural waist.
* Hand Length: Measure from the wrist to the middle finger.
* Hand Width: Measure across the palm of the hand, just under the fingers.
* Foot Length: Measure from toe to heel.
* Foot Circumference: Measure around the ball of the foot.

### Ease

The "ease" of an item indicates how much bigger or smaller than the actual measurements the design is supposed to be worn. Items like hats are designed to be worn with negative ease (slightly smaller than head circumference) so they stay on. Jumpers and cardigans are generally sized with a bit of positive ease (bigger than the actual measurements) so they can be worn over other clothes. Underneath the sizing chart for each pattern is an indication of how much ease the garment is designed to have. If you are making for a baby that hasn't been born yet, think about when the baby is due to arrive and how old they might be when they need the item you are making.

# techniques and basic stitches

## gauge

Everyone crochets differently. Some people work very loosely, some more tightly. To ensure that your garments fit, you need to ensure you are working to the specified gauge. For items such as scarves and home accessories, gauge isn't that critical, as you will just end up with a bigger (or smaller) item. It is worth keeping in mind that gauge that differs from the one specified will also change the amount of yarn you use.

At the most basic level, gauge is the number of stitches and rows in a 4 in square. Each pattern in this book will give you the information as to how many stitches and how many rows it will take to make a 4 in square with your selected yarn and suggested hook.

To see how your gauge matches with the suggested one, make at least a 4 in square with the suggested hook in the indicated stitch pattern. Then, if you plan to wash your finished item, wash and block (see Techniques, page 21) your swatch as you intend to wash your finished object. Let it dry completely and then measure your stitches and rows.

If you measure more stitches and rows in the swatch than the suggested gauge, switch to a larger hook. If you measure fewer stitches and rows in the swatch than the suggested gauge, switch to a smaller hook. Then make another swatch and wash it, as you did the first, to double-check your gauge.

## holding your hook and yarn

Crochet hooks are sometimes held like a pencil, with your forefinger and thumb placed over the flattened portion of the hook, with the end of the hook coming out over your thumb. Others hold their hooks as you would a knife, with the end of the hook under your hand.

.

The yarn should be held in the opposite hand from the hook. It helps to thread the wool through your fingers to create a bit of tension and give you better control of your work.

It will take some time to find what is most comfortable for you. If you are just starting out, choose a project that uses a heavier weight yarn and larger hook, to make it easier to come to grips with the basic techniques.

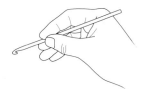

*Hook held like a pencil*

*Hook held like a knife*

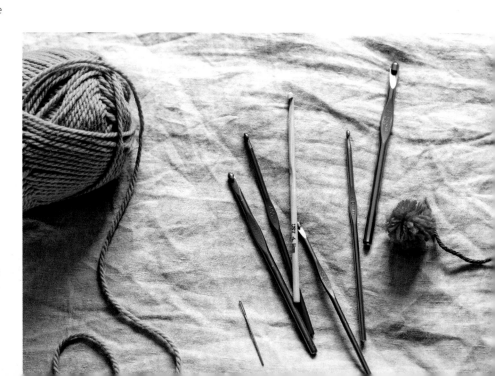

## slip knot

Leaving a 4 in tail, make a loop with the cut end of the yarn behind the ball end of the yarn. Insert your hook into the loop, take the yarn over the hook and pull though. Pull on the tail end of the yarn to tighten the knot.

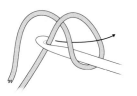

## chain stitch (ch)

Begin with a slip knot on your hook and place your yarn over the hook. Twisting your hook slightly, draw your yarn through the loop on your hook. Repeat as many times as required.

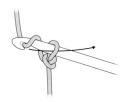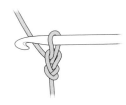

## counting chain stitches

When counting how many stitches you have made, do not count the slip knot at the bottom of the chain or the loop on your hook.

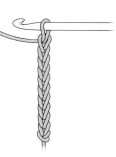

## turning chains (tch)

In order to get your new row or round up to the correct height, you will often be called to make a turning chain. These are chain stitches at the beginning of each row or round. Usually, you count the turning chain as a stitch, except in the case of double crochet. However, each pattern will tell you whether the turning chains are counted or not.

Crochet stitches are different heights. Each stitch has a corresponding number of turning chains made at the beginning of the round/row:

1 ch = Single crochet
2 ch = Half double crochet
3 ch = Double crochet
4 ch = Treble crochet

Sometimes you will be called on to chain more than the number required for the stitch, in which case that will count as a stitch plus a number of chains.

## anatomy of a crochet stitch

**Post**
The "body" of the stitch. This is the portion of the stitch that is made of yarn overs. More yarn overs in a stitch mean a taller post.

**Fork**
This is the bottom portion of the stitch that connects it to the previous round or row.

**Loops**
At the top of the crochet stitch you will see two loops or a "V" that is left after you have made the stitch. Unless otherwise stated, always work into both loops.

**Bar**
Half treble crochet stitches have a horizontal bar that runs at the back of the stitch. In some cases you will work into this instead of the normal Vs of the stitch.

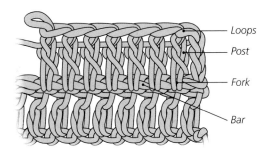

— Loops
— Post
— Fork
— Bar

## slip stitch (sl st)

Slip stitches are most often used for joining rounds or for moving the working yarn to a new point on the garment without having to add bulky stitches or break the yarn.

1. Insert the hook into the stitch.
2. Place the yarn over the hook.
3. Pull through both the stitch and the loop on the hook.

*Moving yarn*

*Joining in the round*

## single crochet (sc)

1. Insert the hook into the stitch.
2. Place the yarn over the hook.
3. Pull through the stitch.
4. Yarn over the hook again.
5. Pull through the two loops on your hook.

## half double crochet (hdc)

1. Place the yarn over the hook.
2. Insert the hook into the stitch.
3. Place the yarn over the hook.
4. Pull through the stitch (three loops on hook).
5. Yarn over the hook again.
6. Pull through all three loops on your hook.

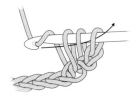

## double crochet (dc)

1. Place the yarn over the hook.
2. Insert the hook into the stitch.
3. Place the yarn over the hook.
4. Pull through the stitch (three loops on hook).
5. Yarn over the hook again.
6. Pull through two loops on your hook (two loops on hook).
7. Yarn over again.
8. Pull through the last two loops on the hook.

## treble crochet (tr)

1. Place the yarn over the hook twice.
2. Insert the hook into the stitch.
3. Place the yarn over the hook.
4. Pull through the stitch (four loops on hook).
5. Yarn over the hook again.
6. Pull through two loops on the hook (three loops on hook).
7. Yarn over the hook again.
8. Pull through two loops on the hook (two loops on hook).
9. Yarn over again.
10. Pull through the last two loops on the hook.

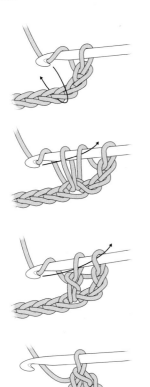

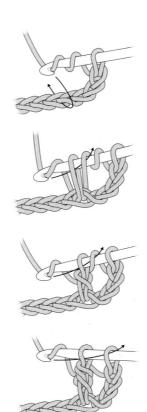

## raised stitches

Raised stitches are used in cable crochet and for making ribbing. They are made by working around the post/body of the stitch, instead of the top of the stitch. Raised stitches can be made with any of the basic stitches, but are most often used with double crochet.

## front post double crochet (fpdc)

**1.** Place the yarn over the hook.

**2.** Insert the hook into the space between the stitch you are raising and the previous stitch, from the front of your work.

**3.** Bring the hook around the back of the stitch and through to the front of your work in between the stitch and the next stitch.

**4.** Yarn over hook.

**5.** Pull the loop back through the spaces between the stitches.

**6.** Yarn over and pull through two loops twice, as you would a normal double crochet.

## back post double crochet (bpdc)

**1.** Place the yarn over the hook.

**2.** Bring the hook to the back of your work and insert the hook into the space between the stitch you are raising and the previous stitch, from the back of your work.

**3.** Bring the hook around the front of the stitch and through to the back of your work in between the stitch and the next stitch.

**4.** Yarn over hook.

**5.** Pull the loop back through the spaces between the stitches.

**6.** Yarn over and pull through two loops twice, as you would a normal double crochet.

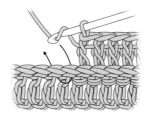
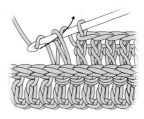
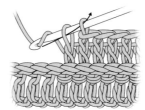
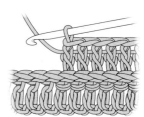

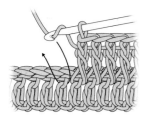
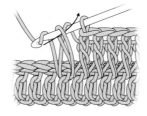
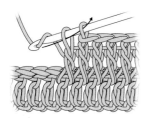
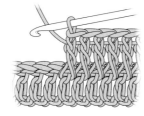

## cabled crochet

Cables are achieved in crochet by crossing groups of post stitches. It can be tricky to understand at first. In all of the cables worked in this book, you will skip a specified number of stitches, work a group of post stitches, then go back and work the missed stitches so they cross over the front of the cable. You then continue working as normal in the pattern.

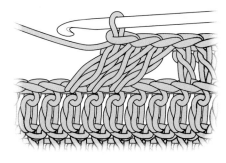

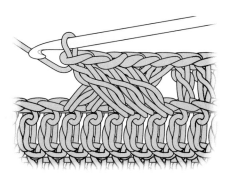

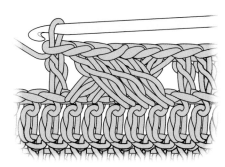

## foundation single crochet (fsc)

Foundation crochet or chainless crochet is a way of working a starting row without having to work a chain. This is used in places where you need more stretch than a chain stitch can provide.

**1.** Starting with a slip knot, chain two.

**2.** Insert your hook back into the first chain.

**3.** Yarn over and pull through (two loops on hook). This links your stitches together.

**4.** Yarn over and pull through one loop on your hook (two loops on hook). This counts as your chain stitch.

**5.** Yarn over again and pull through the remaining two loops on your hook.

To continue:

**1.** Insert your hook into the chain stitch of the previous fsc.

**2.** Yarn over and pull through (two loops on hook). This counts as your joining stitch.

**3.** Yarn over and pull through one loop on your hook (two loops on hook). This counts as your chain stitch.

**4.** Yarn over again and pull through the remaining two loops on the hook.

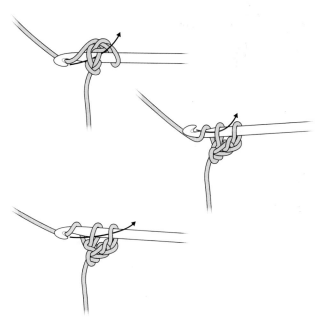

## foundation double crochet (fdc)

**1.** Starting with a slip knot, chain three.

**2.** Yarn over.

**3.** Insert the hook back into the first chain made.

**4.** Yarn over and pull through chain (three loops on hook). This links your stitches together.

**5.** Yarn over and pull through one loop on your hook (three loops on hook). This counts as your new chain stitch.

**6.** Yarn over and pull through two loops.

**7.** Yarn over again and pull through the remaining two loops on the hook.

To continue:

**1.** Yarn over.

**2.** Insert your hook into the chain stitch of the previous fdc.

**3.** Yarn over and pull through chain (three loops on hook). This links your stitches together.

**4.** Yarn over and pull through one loop on your hook (three loops on hook). This counts as your new chain stitch.

**5.** Yarn over and pull through two loops.

**6.** Yarn over again and pull through the remaining two loops on your hook.

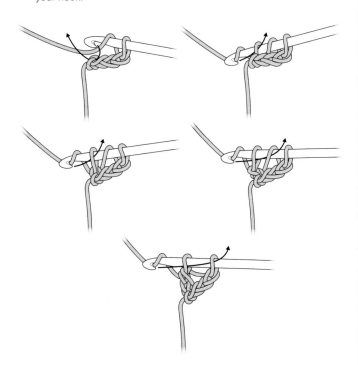

## decreases

Decreases are made by working the specified stitch up to the last yarn over, then inserting the hook into the next stitch and working it up to the last yarn over. Then yarn over and pull through all the loops on your hook. This is often written in the pattern as 2tog.

## single crochet two together (sc2tog)

**1.** Insert hook into the next stitch.

**2.** Yarn over and pull through.

Work steps 1 and 2 twice.

**3.** Yarn over and pull through all of the loops on your hook.

1 single crochet stitch decreased.

## working in the round

One of the neatest ways to start working in rounds is with a magic loop (also called adjustable loop). This is my preferred way of starting, as it enables you to get a very tight, closed first round.

**1.** Make a loop with the yarn, placing the cut end behind the ball end of the yarn.

**2.** Pinch the loop where the yarn crosses, holding the loop secure.

**3.** Insert your hook into the big loop.

**4.** Chain the specified number of stitches, using your magic loop as a slip stitch. This will help secure the loop.

**5.** Make the specified stitches, working around the loop.

**6.** Pull the tail end tightly to bring the bottom of the stitches into a circle.

**7.** After you have worked a few rounds of the pattern, tie off the tail end to prevent the magic loop from opening back up.

## Tunisian crochet

Tunisian or Afghan crochet is a method that is worked with a crochet hook with a flexible cord attached to the end. Tunisian is worked in long rows, always with the right side facing. Each row has two distinct parts—the forward pass and the return pass. This book only uses two of the most basic Tunisian stitches and gives a great introduction to this incredibly versatile method of crochet.

### set-up row (this is the same for all Tunisian stitches) forward pass:

**1.** Chain a length, starting with the second chain from the hook.

**2.** Insert the hook into the chain, yarn over and pull through. Work step 2 until all chains have been worked. You will have as many loops on your hook as you have chain stitches, excluding the first chain you missed.

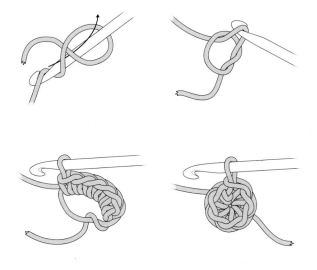

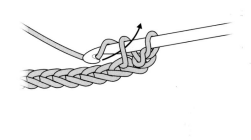

Alternatively, if you find the magic loop difficult, you can begin working in the round with four chains. Join with a slip stitch in the round and work your pattern into the loop created by the ring of chain stitched (not working into the individual chains, as you would when working flat).

## standard return pass (srp)

**1.** Yarn over and pull through one loop on hook (this is the equivalent of your turning chain).

**2.** Yarn over and pull through two loops on the hook.

Work step 2 until only one loop remains on the hook.

## Tunisian simple stitch (tss)

After working a set-up row and standard return pass:

**1.** Insert the hook into the next vertical bar created by the previous row.

**2.** Yarn over and pull through.

Work steps 1 and 2 to the end of the row.

**3.** Insert the hook into the chain at the end of the row, yarn over and pull through.

Work a standard return pass to close off your stitches.

## Tunisian knit stitch (tks)

After working a set-up row and standard return pass:

**1.** Insert the hook from front to back, through your fabric, immediately to the right of the vertical bar created by the previous row.

**2.** Yarn over and pull through.

**3.** Work steps 1 and 2 to the end of the row.

**4.** Insert your hook into the chain at the end of the row, yarn over and pull through.

Work a standard return pass to close off your stitches.

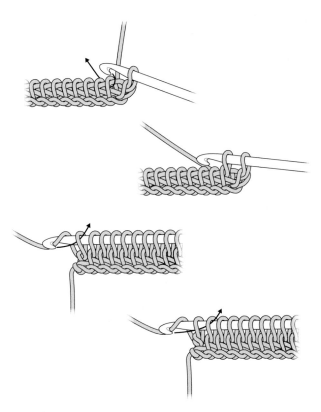

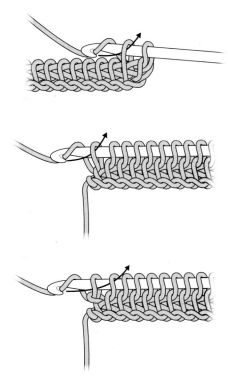

## reading Tunisian patterns

Tunisian crochet patterns are read like other crochet patterns, but each row will give instructions for both the forward and return passes.

## joining yarns

To join a new color or ball of yarn seamlessly to your work, switch your yarn at the last yarn over of the stitch. For example, if I were switching when using single crochet, I would:

1. Insert the hook into the stitch.
2. Place the yarn over the hook.
3. Pull through the stitch.
4. Yarn over the hook again with the new color/yarn.
5. Pull through the two loops on the hook.

You can easily work in any ends of yarn, by working around them as you continue along the round/row. Simply lay them across the top of the row you are working on and continue crocheting into the stitches as normal.

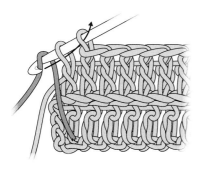

## finishing

Once you reach the end of your work, cut the yarn, leaving at least a 6 in tail for weaving in. Pull the cut end through the last loop that remained on the hook to stop your stitches from unraveling. If there are yarn ends that you have not been able to work in as described above, use a tapestry needle to weave the remaining end securely into the back of your work. Weaving them into three or four stitches in three or four different directions will ensure they do not pop out later.

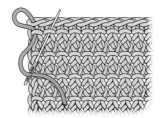 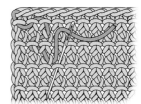

## washing and blocking

Always use the ball band for your yarn as a guide to how to care for your finished item. Many will say "Hand Wash Only"; however if your machine has it, it is often OK to use a wool cycle on most handmade items. Test your swatch first. It's a good idea to include a note on the washing instructions along with your gift.

When working with wools that have a high natural fiber content, you can block your project, which will help the yarn relax into the shape you have made. There are many different blocking techniques. Steam blocking uses an iron with a high steam setting. Press your work gently (not too hard or you will flatten the stitches).

Wet blocking can take longer to dry, but does tend to give most consistent results.

**1.** Wet your work in lukewarm water with a bit of wool wash in it.

**2.** Gently agitate your work.

**3.** Rinse your work in cool water and gently press the water out.

**4.** Place your work flat on a towel and roll it up to get more water out.

**5.** Lay the item out on a flat surface. Pin down the edges in shape using pins that won't rust.

**6.** Leave to fully dry.

## sewing up

### Slip Stitch Seams

Using a slipstitch to join different parts of an object creates a very strong seam. Line up the stitches of the two pieces you are joining and insert your hook through all four loops of the stitches on both pieces, yarn over hook, and pull through the loop on your hook through the two pieces you are joining. Repeat to the end of the seam.

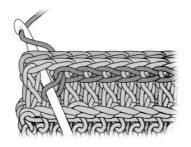

### Running Stitch

Thread the needle with yarn and work up and down through the crochet fabric with even spaces between the stitches.

### Backstitch

Backstitch is similar to running stitch, except you work some of the stitches back on themselves. Pull the stitch through the crochet fabric and then back into the underside behind where the thread came out. The needle is carried under the fabric to the far point of the new stitch, where it is brought up again and back to where the thread was brought up on the last stitch.

### Whipstitch

Lining up your stitches, insert your threaded needle from the right side of the first stitch on the bottom piece and through the adjoining first stitch on the top piece from the wrong side. Bring your needle over the top of your work and back to the bottom piece, working into each stitch as above.

## making a pompom

**1.** Cut a 12 in length of contrast yarn and set it aside.

**2.** Using the yarn still attached to the ball, secure the cut end of yarn between two fingers of your non-dominant hand and wrap it around them until it is at least 1in thick (use more fingers for a big pompom and two for a small one).

**3.** Carefully remove the yarn from your fingers.

**4.** Pick up the set-aside yarn and wrap it widthwise around the loops of yarn. Tie it off tightly.

**5.** Cut the loops, being careful not to cut the securing tie. Fluff up the yarn and trim into a pompom shape.

## reading a pattern

Reading a pattern can be like reading a code. It can be tricky at first, but patterns are written using standard abbreviations for stitches and what to do. Know the code and you've got it!

| Stitch or instruction | Abbreviation |
|---|---|
| Back Loop Only | BLO |
| Back Post | BPxx (xx can be any stitch) |
| Beginning Chain | Beg ch |
| Between | bet |
| Centimeter(s) | cm |
| Chain | ch |
| Chain Space | ch-space |
| Double Crochet | dc |
| Double Treble Crochet | dtr |
| Foundation Single Crochet | fsc |
| Foundation Double Crochet | fdc |
| Front Post | FPxx (xx can be any stitch) |
| Half Double Crochet | hdc |
| Inch(es) | in |
| Increasing | inc |
| Place Marker | pm |
| Remove Marker | rm |
| Single Crochet | sc |
| Slip Marker (move the marker up a row) | sm |
| Slip stitch | sl st |
| Space | sp |
| Stitches | sts |
| Treble Crochet | tr |
| Turning Chain | t-ch |
| Work 2 xx Together | xx2tog (xx can be any stitch) |
| Yarn Over | YO |
| Yard(s) | yd |

## Pattern Basics

Example: Rows 1–2 (3, 4, 5): Ch 1, [2 sc in sc, 2 sc] three times, 2 (3, 4, 5) sc, *2 sc in sc; repeat from * to end. Join. Turn. 20 (21, 22, 23) sts.

✳ Numbers in round brackets ( ) relate to the instructions for the various sizes from smallest to largest, working left to right. They can be row or round numbers, stitch counts or repeats.

✳ The instruction "2 sc in sc, 2 sc," means make two single crochet in the next single crochet stitch, then single crochet in each of the next two stitches.

✳ Instructions in square brackets [ ] are to be repeated a set number of times, as directed immediately following the second bracket. There may be variations relating to the size, in which case follow the appropriate number in round brackets.

✳ "Join" means join the round.

✳ "Turn" means turn your work.

✳ The stitch counts at the end of the row tell you how many stitches you should have worked in that row or round.

✳ "Work even" means continue in the stitch pattern as presented.

# For the home

\* \* \* \* \* \* \*

# cabled throw

Thick and warm yarn, chunky cables—this large throw is deliciously soft and perfect for curling up under (even when you are making it).

## skill level **intermediate**

| Size | One size |
| --- | --- |
| Finished width | 37 in |
| Finished length | 59 in |
| Yarn amount | 1676 yd |

### materials:
* 17 x 3½ oz balls of Drops Andes (65% wool, 35% alpaca), Color 0100
* M/13 hook

### yarn review:
Fluffy like a cloud, this super chunky yarn makes a quick and gorgeous throw.

### yarn alternatives:
Cascade Magnum

### gauge:
Work 9 sts and 11 rows in single crochet to measure 4 in square using M/13 hook, or size needed to achieve gauge.

### special stitches:

**Baby Cable**

**Row 1:** Skip next st, 1FPtr one row below next st, 1FPtr one row below missed st.

**Row 2 and all WS rows:** Sc across. Repeat Rows 1–2 as called for in the pattern.

**Three Stitch Cable**

**Row 1:** Skip next st, [1FPtr one row below next st] twice, 1FPtr one row below missed st.

**Row 2 and all WS rows:** Sc across.

**Row 3, 5 and 7:** [1fpdc one row below next stitch] three times.

**Six Stitch Cable**

**Row 1:** [1fpdc one row below next st] six times.

**Row 2 and all WS rows:** Sc across.

**Row 3:** Rep Row 1.

**Row 5:** Skip next 3 sts, [1FPtr one row below next st] three times, 1FPtr one row below each missed st.

**Row 7:** Rep Row 1.

### pattern note:
Do not count the turning chain as a stitch.

## instructions:

Chain 83.

### Edging

**Row 1:** Starting in fourth ch from hook, 80dc. Turn. 80 sts.

**Rows 2–3:** Ch 2, *1 fpdc, 1 bpdc; rep from * across. Turn.

**Row 4:** Ch 1, 80sc. Turn.

### Cable Pattern

**Row 1:** Ch 1, [2 sc, work Row 1 of Baby Cable, 2 sc, work Row 1 of Three Stitch Cable, 2 sc, work Row 1 of Six Stitch Cable, 2 sc, work Row 1 of Three Stitch Cable, 2 sc, work Row 1 of Baby Cable] three times, 2 sc. Turn.

**Row 2 and all WS rows:** Ch 1, sc across.

**Row 3:** Ch 1, [2 sc, work Row 1 of Baby Cable, 2 sc, work Row 3 of Three Stitch Cable, 2 sc, work Row 3 of Six Stitch Cable, 2 sc, work Row 3 of Three Stitch Cable, 2 sc, work Row 1 of Baby Cable] three times, 2 sc. Turn.

**Row 5:** Ch 1, [2 sc, work Row 1 of Baby Cable, 2 sc, work Row 5 of Three Stitch Cable, 2 sc, work Row 5 of Six Stitch Cable, 2 sc, work Row 5 of Three Stitch Cable, 2 sc, work Row 5 of Baby Cable] three times, 2 sc. Turn.

**Row 7:** Ch 1, [2 sc, work Row 1 of Baby Cable, 2 sc, work Row 7 of Three Stitch Cable, 2 sc, work Row 7 of Six Stitch Cable, 2 sc, work Row 7 of Three Stitch Cable, 2 sc, work Row 7 of Baby Cable] three times, 2 dc. Turn.

**Rows 9–120:** Work Rows 1–8 a further 14 times. The pattern is worked 15 times in total.

### Edging

**Row 1:** Ch3, 80hdc. Turn.

**Rows 2–4:** Ch3, 1fpdc, 1bpdc; rep from * across. Turn.

### Finishing

Weave in the ends.

Block to size.

*For a different look, work the ribbing in a contrasting color.*

# cabled cushion

Cloud-like alpaca wool blend yarn creates a squishy cabled cushion—a perfect dream.

## skill level **intermediate**

| Size | One size |
|---|---|
| Finished width | 16 in |
| Finished length | 16 in |
| Yarn amount | 402 yd |

### materials:

* 4 x 3½ oz balls of Drops Andes (65% wool, 35% alpaca), Color 0100
* M/13 hook
* 16 in square cushion pad

### yarn review:

This is the softest super bulky yarn I know of—beautifully soft, it comes in a gorgeous range of colors and is very affordable.

### yarn alternative:

Cascade Magnum

### gauge:

Work 9 sts and 11 rows in single crochet to measure 4 in sqaure using M/13 hook, or size needed to achieve gauge.

## special stitches:

### Baby Cable

**Row 1:** Skip next st, 1FPtr one row below next st, 1FPtr one row below missed st.

**Row 2 and all WS rows:** Sc across.

Repeat Rows 1–2 as called for in the pattern.

### Three Stitch Cable

**Row 1:** [1FPtr one row below next st] three times.

**Row 2 and all WS rows:** Sc across.

**Row 3:** Skip next st, [1FPtr one row below next st] twice, 1FPtr one row below skipped stitch.

**Row 5:** Rep Row 1.

### Six Stitch Cable

**Row 1:** [1FPtr one row below next st] six times.

**Row 2 and all WS rows:** Sc across.

**Row 3:** Rep Row 1.

**Row 5:** Skip next 3 sts, [1FPtr one row below next st] three times, 1FPtr one row below each skipped st.

Work Rows 1–6 a total of 11 times.

### pattern note:

Do not count the turning chain as a stitch.

## instructions:

Chain 39.

### Ribbing

**Row 1:** Starting in fourth ch from hook, 36 dc. Turn. 36 sts.

**Rows 2–4:** Ch2, *1fpdc, 1bpdc; rep from * across. Turn.

### Cable Pattern

**Row 1:** Ch 1, 6 sc, work Row 1 of Baby Cable, 2 sc, work Row 1 of Three Stitch Cable, 2 sc, work Row 1 of Six Stitch Cable, 2 sc, work Row 1 of Three Stitch Cable, 2 sc, work Row 1 of Baby Cable, 6 sc. Turn.

**Row 2 and all WS rows:** Ch 1, sc across.

**Row 3:** Ch 1, 6 sc, work Row 1 of Baby Cable, 2 sc, work Row 3 of Three Stitch Cable, 2 sc, work Row 3 of Six Stitch Cable, 2 sc, work Row 3 of Three Stitch Cable, 2 sc, work Row 1 of Baby Cable, 6 sc. Turn.

**Row 5:** Ch 1, 6 sc, work Row 1 of Baby Cable, 2 sc, work Row 5 of Three Stitch Cable, 2 sc, work Row 5 of Six Stitch Cable, 2 sc, work Row 5 of Three Stitch Cable, 2 sc, work Row 1 of Baby Cable, 6 sc. Turn.

**Row 7:** Ch 1, 6 sc, work Row 1 of Baby Cable, 2 sc, work Row 7 of Three Stitch Cable, 2 sc, work Row 7 of Six Stitch Cable, 2 sc, work Row 7 of Three Stitch Cable, 2 sc, work Row 1 of Baby Cable, 6 sc. Turn.

Work Rows 1–8 a total of seven times.

### Ribbing

**Row 1:** Ch3, 36 dc. Turn.

**Rows 2–4:** Ch3, 1fpdc, 1bpdc; rep from * across. Turn.

### Finishing

With right sides facing, fold the cushion cover so that the short ends of the ribbing overlap by 4 in. Sew up the sides of the cushion cover. Turn right side out and insert the cushion pad.

This is a complementary cable pattern to the Cabled Throw, so make it in the same color for a set.

# *kitschy koo potholders*

These retro-inspired, embroidered potholders with their double layer are as practical as they are beautiful. And there's a choice of two designs.

## skill level **beginner**

| Size | One size |
|------|----------|
| Finished size | 7 in square |
| Yarn amount (Color A) | 120 yd |
| Yarn amount (Color B) | 22 yd |
| Yarn amount (Color C) | 22 yd |

## materials:

* Color A: 1 x 1¾ oz ball of Rico Essentials Cotton DK (100% cotton), Nature (51)
* Color B: 1 x 1¾ oz ball of Rico Essentials Cotton DK (100% cotton), Dusky Rose (51)
* Color C: 1 x 1¾ oz ball of Rico Essentials Cotton DK (100% cotton), Berry (51)
* G/6 hook

## yarn review:

This mercerized sport weight cotton comes in a rainbow of colors.

## yarn alternative:

James C Brett Cotton On

## gauge:

Work 19 sts and 20 rows in double crochet to measure 4 in square using G/6 hook, or size needed to achieve gauge.

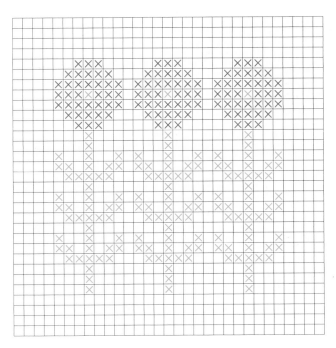

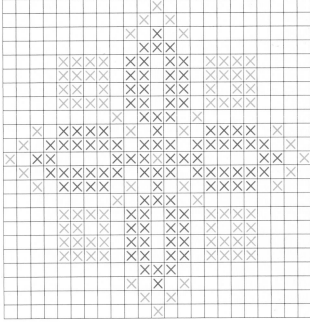

*Blocking first opens out the stitches and makes the fabric much easier to embroider.*

## pattern (make 2 for each potholder):

In Color A, ch 32.

**Row 1:** Starting in second ch from hook, 31 sc.

**Rows 2–31:** Ch 1, 31 sc.

### Embroidery

Wash and dry the squares. Using each stitch as a square on the chart, embroider one of the squares with your choice of design.

### Finishing

Place the embroidered square right side up on top of the plain square. With the embroidered square facing, attach Color B at the top left-hand corner. Working through both layers, sc in each stitch and row around the square, working 3 sts into the stitch at the corners and sl st to join. Without turning, attach Color C, ch 15, 1 sc in the stitch corner stitch, 1 sc in each stitch around the square, 3 sc in each corner stitch. When you reach the chain, work 1 sc into each ch and sl st to finish. Weave in ends.

# linen snowflakes and stars

Tiny and delicate, these linen motifs make a beautiful addition to holiday décor. String them for a garland, use them in giftwrapping or put them on the Christmas tree.

## skill level **beginner**

|  | Snowflake | Star |
|---|---|---|
| Finished width | 3½ in | 3½ in |
| Yarn amount | 14 yd | 11 yd |

### materials:
* 1 x 1¾ oz ball of 3-ply Linen Thread (100% wetspun linen), White
* D/3 hook

### yarn review:
This lace-weight linen thread holds its shape without blocking.

### yarn alternative:
DMC Petra 3

### gauge:
1 motif measures 3½ in wide.

### special stitches:
**Bobble Stitch (BS)**
[YO, insert the hook into the stitch, YO and pull through the stitch, YO and pull through two loops] three times, YO and pull through all the loops on your hook.

**Triple Picot (tr pic)**
Ch 5, sl st into the first chain, [ch 5, sl st into the same chain as the first sl st] twice.

**Picot (pic)**
Ch 5, sl st into the first chain made.

## pattern notes:

Do not count the beginning chain as a stitch.
Work with the RS facing.

*Linen thread can be tricky to work with, but its structure really helps these little flakes keep their shape.*

## snowflake instructions:

**Rnd 1:** Working into magic loop (see Techniques, page 17), ch 1, 6 sc. Join.

**Rnd 2:** Ch3, [1BS, ch 2] six times. Join. 6 sts.

**Rnd 3:** 2sl st to next ch-space, [(2BS, ch 3, 2BS, ch 1) into next ch-space, skip 1BS] six times. Join. 24 sts.

**Rnd 4:** Ch 1, [skip 2BS, (2BS, 1tr pic, 2BS) into next ch-space, skip 2BS, 1 sc into ch1-space] six times. Join. 30 sts.

## star instructions:

**Rnd 1:** Working into magic loop, ch 1, 5 sc. Join.

**Rnd 2:** Ch3, [1BS, ch 2] five times. Join. 5 sts.

**Rnd 3:** 2sl st to next ch-space, [(ch 3, 2BS, ch 3, 2BS, ch 1) into next ch-space, skip 1BS], five times. Join. 20 sts.

**Rnd 4:** Ch 1, [skip 2BS, (2BS, 1pic, 2BS) into next ch-space, skip 2BS, 1 sc into ch1-space] five times. 25 sts.

## instructions:

Block lightly. For the best results, pin each of the picot points to let them dry into shape. To make bunting, ch 20, [1 sc into the central picot point on one snowflake, ch 25]. Repeat for as many snowflakes as you have made.

# christmas wreath

These wreaths are quick and addictive to make.

## skill level **beginner**

|  | Wreath ornaments | Large wreaths |
| --- | --- | --- |
| Finished wreath circumference | 2 in | 12 in |
| Yarn amount (wreath) | 11 yd | 55 yd |
| Yarn amount (bow) | 6 yd | 11 yd |

Photos show large size.

## materials:

**For Wreath Ornament**

* 1 x 1¾ oz ball of Rico Creative Cotton (100% cotton), White (Wreath)
* 1 x 1¾ oz ball of Rico Creative Cotton (100% cotton), Red (Bow)
* 1 x 1½ in diameter curtain hoop per ornament
* E/4 hook

**For Large Wreath**

* 1 x 3½ oz ball Texere Chunky Wool (100% wool), White (Wreath)
* 1 x 3½ oz ball Texere Chunky Wool (100% wool), Red (Bow)
* 8 in embroidery hoop
* Small amount of ribbon for hanging
* I/9 hook

## yarn review:

Both of the yarns for the wreath have excellent stitch definition and a good amount of structure to ensure the wreath is held open.

## yarn alternative:

This pattern is easily adapted to use any yarn you may have to hand.

## gauge:

Gauge isn't crucial to this pattern, but use a small enough hook to achieve a tight tension.

## pattern note:

If your gauge or hoop size is different from the pattern, simply ensure you are using a multiple of three in Rnd 1 and work the remaining rounds from there.

## instructions:

With yarn for the wreath, start with a slip knot on your hook. Insert the hook through the hoop just next to the screw fitting, YO and pull through the hoop and the loop on the hook to secure the yarn to the hoop.

**Rnd 1:** Working around the hoop, 51 (81) sc around. Join round by making sl st into 1st sc of round, working in front of screw fitting.

**Rnd 2:** Ch 1, *1 sc, ch 3, skip 2 sts; rep from *around. Do not join. 17 (27) ch-space.

**Rnd 3:** 1 sc into first ch-space, ch 4. *1 sc into next ch-space, ch 4; rep from * around. Do not join.

**Rnd 4:** 1 sc into first ch-space, ch 5. *1 sc into the next ch-space, ch 5; rep from * around.

Do not join.

Break yarn.

### Bow

Using yarn for the bow, leaving a 1½ in tail, ch 30. Join the chain into a loop.

**Rnd 1:** Ch 1, 30sc. Do not join.

Work Rnd 1 a total of six times. Cut your yarn, leaving a 18 in tail.

Align the tails in the center of the bow. Use the long tail to wrap around the middle of the bow until you are left with a 3 in tail. Use the tails to secure the bow to the wreath.

### Finishing

Block and pin the wreath to help it keep its shape. Spray starch may also help. Tie a piece of ribbon to the screw fitting for hanging.

*By no means limited to Christmas, use different colors for every season.*

# pouf and it's gone

Hide extra blankets in this patterned pouf.
A removable cover means that you can take
the pouf apart for washing.

## skill level **beginner**

| **Size** | One size |
| --- | --- |
| Diameter | 76 in |
| Yarn amount | 263 yd |

**materials:**
* 3 x 17½ oz cones of Fireside Yarn T-shirt
  Yarn (100% cotton jersey), Purple
  Passion
* M/13 hook
* 1 double duvet with cover or large
  blanket (cover shows through the pouf,
  so pick complementary colors)

**yarn review:**
Working to a super bulky-weight, T-shirt
yarn comes in every color of the rainbow.

**yarn alternative:**
Hoopla T-shirt Yarn

**gauge:**
Work 8 sts and 3 rows in double crochet to
measure 4 in square using M/13 hook, or
size needed to achieve tension.

**pattern notes:**
Count the ch 3 at the beginning of the
round as a stitch.
The pattern is worked without turning,
RS facing.

next dc and ch-space, 2 dc in next dc, 1 dc, 2 dc in next dc, skip next dc, ch 3, skip ch3-space and next dc, 2 dc, 2 dc in next dc, ch 3, [2 dc in next dc, 2 dc, ch 3, skip next dc and ch-space, 2 dc in next dc, 1 dc, 2 dc in next dc, skip next dc, ch 3, skip ch3-space and next dc, 2 dc, 2 dc in next dc, ch 3] six times. Join. 91 dc.

**Rnd 10:** Ch3, 1 dc in same st, 2 dc, ch 3, skip next dc and ch-space, 2 dc in next dc, 1 dc, ch 3, skip next dc, 1 dc, 2 dc in next dc, skip next dc, ch 3, skip ch3-space and next dc, 2 dc, 2 dc in next dc, ch 3, [2 dc in next

**instructions:**

**Rnd 1:** Working into magic loop (see Techniques, page 17), ch 6 (counts as 1 dc and ch 3), [1 dc, ch 3] six times. Join. 7 dc.

**Rnd 2:** Ch3, 1 dc in same st, ch 3, [2 dc in next dc, ch 3] six times. Join. 14 dc.

**Rnd 3:** Ch3, 1 dc in same st, 1 dc, ch 3, [2 dc in next dc, 1 dc, ch 3] six times. Join. 21 dc.

**Rnd 4:** Ch3, 1 dc in same st, 1 dc, 2 dc in next dc, ch 3, [2 dc in next dc, 1 dc, 2 dc in next dc, ch 3] six times. Join. 35 dc.

**Rnd 5:** Ch3, 1 dc in same st, 3 dc, 2 dc in next dc, ch 3, [2 dc in next dc, 3 dc, 2 dc in next dc, ch 3] six times. Join. 49 dc.

**Rnd 6:** Ch3, 1 dc in same st, 2 dc, ch 3, skip next dc, 2 dc, 2 dc in next dc, ch 3, [2 dc in next dc, 2 dc, ch 3, skip next dc, 2 dc, 2 dc in next dc, ch 3] six times. Join. 56 dc.

**Rnd 7:** Ch3, 1 dc in same st, 2 dc, ch 3, skip next dc, 1 dc in ch3-space, ch 3, skip next dc, 2 dc, 2 dc in next dc, ch 3, [2 dc in next dc, 2 dc, ch 3, skip next dc, 1 dc in ch3-space, ch 3, skip next dc, 2 dc, 2 dc in next dc, ch 3] six times. Join. 63 dc.

**Rnd 8:** Ch3, 1 dc in same st, 2 dc, ch 3, skip next dc, 1 dc in ch-space, 1 dc in dc, 1 dc in ch-space, ch 3, skip next dc, 2 dc, 2 dc in next dc, ch 3, [2 dc in next dc, 2 dc, ch 3, skip next dc, 1 dc in ch-space, 1 dc in dc, 1 dc in ch-space, ch 3, skip next dc, 2 dc, 2 dc in next dc, ch 3] six times. Join. 77 dc.

**Rnd 9:** Ch3, 1 dc in same st, 2 dc, ch 3, skip

dc, 2 dc, ch 3, skip next dc and ch-space, 2 dc in next dc, 1 dc, skip next dc, ch 3, 1 dc, 2 dc in next dc, skip next dc, ch 3, skip next ch-space and dc, 2 dc, 2 dc in next dc, ch 3] six times. Join. 98 dc.

**Rnd 11:** Ch3, 3 dc, ch 3, skip next ch-space and dc, 2 dc, 1 dc into ch-space, 2 dc, ch 3, skip next dc and ch-space, 4 dc, ch 3 [4 dc, ch 3, skip ch-space and next dc, 2 dc, 1 dc into ch-space, 2 dc, skip next dc and ch-space, ch 3, 4 dc, ch 3] six times. Join. 91 dc.

**Rnd 12:** Ch3, 3 dc, ch 3, skip ch-space and next dc, 3 dc, ch 3, skip next dc and ch-space, 4 dc, ch 3 [4 dc, ch 3, skip next dc and ch-space, 3 dc, ch 3, skip next dc and ch-space, 4 dc, ch 3] six times. Join. 77 dc.

**Rnd 13:** Ch3, 3 dc, ch 3, skip ch-space and next dc, 1 dc, skip next dc and ch-space, ch 3, 4 dc, ch 3 [4 dc, ch 3, skip next dc and ch-space, 1 dc, skip next dc and ch-space, ch 3, 4 dc, ch 3] six times. Join. 63 dc.

**Rnd 14:** Ch3, 3 dc, ch 3, skip ch-space and next dc, 4 dc, ch 3 [4 dc, ch 3, skip next dc and ch-space, 4 dc, ch 3] six times. Join. 56 dc.

**Rnd 15:** Ch3, 1 dc2tog, 1 dc, 1 dc in ch-space, 2 dc, 1 dc2tog, ch 3, [1dc2tog, 2 dc, 1 dc in ch-space, 2 dc, 1 dc2tog, ch 3] six times. Join. 49 dc.

**Rnd 16:** Ch3, 1 dc2tog, 2 dc, 1 dc2tog, ch 3, [1 dc2tog, 3 dc, 1 dc2tog, ch 3] six times. Join. 35 dc. Break yarn.

## Removable Cover

**Rnd 1:** Working into magic loop, ch 6 (counts as 1 dc and ch 3), [1 dc, ch 3] six times. Join. 7 dc.

**Rnd 2:** Ch3, 1 dc in same stitch, ch 3, [2 dc in next dc, ch 3] six times. Join. 14 dc.

**Rnd 3:** Ch3, 2 dc in next dc, ch 3, [1 dc, 2 dc in next dc, ch 3] six times. Join. 21 dc.

**Rnd 4:** Ch3, 1 dc, 2 dc in next dc, ch 3, [2 dc, 2 dc in next dc, ch 3] six times. Join. 28 dc.

**Rnd 5:** Ch3, 2 dc, 2 dc in next dc, ch 3, [3 dc, 2 dc in next dc, ch 3] six times. Join. 35 dc.

**Rnd 6:** Ch3, 3 dc, 2 dc in next dc, ch 3, [4 dc, 2 dc in next dc, ch 3] six times. Join. 42 dc.

Break yarn and weave in the ends.

## Finishing

Stuff the pouf with the duvet or blanket. Insert the removable cover inside the pouf to keep it secured.

# color block baskets

These hard-wearing baskets make a great gift on their own
or as storage for other things.

## skill level **beginner**

| Size | Small | Medium | Large | Extra large |
|---|---|---|---|---|
| Diameter | 7 in | 9½ in | 12 in | 14¼ in |
| Height | 7 in | 9½ in | 12 in | 14¼ in |
| Yarn amount (MC) | 66 yd | 109 yd | 175 yd | 252 yd |
| Yarn amount (CC) | 99 yd | 175 yd | 274 yd | 383 yd |

Photos show small size.

### materials:

* Main Color (MC): 1 (1, 1, 1) spool of
  3-ply Nutscene Fillis Natural Jute Twine
  (100% jute), Fillis
* Contrast Color (CC): 1 (2, 2, 3) balls
  of 3-ply Nutscene Heritage Range
  Colorful Jute Twine (100% jute), Marine,
  Terracotta
* I/9 hook

### yarn review:

This garden twine comes in every
color imaginable and lends itself well to
home projects.

### yarn alternative:

Any twine or cotton string will work, but a
change in gauge may result in a change in
quantity needed.

### gauge:

Work 12 sts and 10 rows in double crochet
to measure 4 in square using I/9 hook, or size
needed to achieve gauge.

### pattern note:

Do not count the t-ch at the beginning of
the round as a stitch.

*Be careful when blocking the baskets, as the dye on some colored twines can bleed.*

### instructions:

**Rnd 1:** Working into a magic loop (see Techniques, page 17) and CC, ch 1, 8 sc. Join. 8 sts.

**Rnd 2:** Ch 1, *2 sc into next st; rep from * around. Join. 16 sts.

**Rnd 3:** Ch 1, *1 sc, 2 sc into next st; rep from * around. Join. 24 sts.

**Rnd 4:** Ch 1, *2 sc, 2 sc into next st; rep from * around. Join. 32 sts.

**Rnd 5:** Ch 1, *3 sc, 2 sc into next st st; rep from * around. Join. 40 sts.

**Rnd 6:** Ch 1, *4 sc, 2 sc into next st; rep from * around. Join. 48 sts.

**Rnd 7:** Ch 1, *5 sc, 2 sc into next st; rep from * around. Join. 56 sts.

**Rnd 8:** Ch 1, *6 sc, 2 sc into next st; rep from * around. Join. 64 sts.

**Rnd 9:** Ch 1, *7 sc, 2 sc into next st; rep from* around. Join. 72 sts.

For size Small, continue to Sides.

**For sizes Medium, Large and Extra Large ONLY**

**Rnd 10:** Ch 1, *8 sc, 2 sc into next st; rep from * around. Join. 80 sts.

**Rnd 11:** Ch 1, *9 sc, 2 sc into next st; rep from * around. Join. 88 sts.

**Rnd 12:** Ch 1, *10sc, 2 sc into next st; rep from * around. Join. 96 sts.

For size Medium, continue to Sides.

**For sizes Large and Extra Large ONLY**

**Rnd 13:** Ch 1, *11 sc, 2 sc into next st; rep from * around. Join. 104 sts.

**Rnd 14:** Ch 1, *12 sc, 2 sc into next st; rep from * around. Join. 112 sts.

**Rnd 15:** Ch 1, *13 sc, 2 sc into next st; rep from * around. Join. 120 sts.

For size Large, continue to Sides.

**For size Extra Large ONLY**
**Rnd 16:** Ch 1, *14 sc, 2 sc into next st; rep from * around. Join. 128 sts.
**Rnd 17:** Ch 1, *15 sc, 2 sc into next st; rep from * around. Join. 136 sts.
**Rnd 18:** Ch 1, *16 sc, 2 sc into next st; rep from * around. Join. 144 sts.

**Sides**
Work 8 (11, 14, 17) rounds even in sc with CC, switch to MC and work 5 (8, 11, 14) rounds even in sc.

**Handles**
**Rnd 1 (32, 40, 49):** Ch 1, 12 (18, 24, 30) ssc, 12 sc, skip next 12 sc, 24 (36, 48, 60) sc, 12 sc, skip next 12 sc, 12 (18, 24, 30) sc. Join. 48 (72, 96, 120) sts.
**Rnds 2–5 (32–35, 41–44, 50–53):** Ch 1, 72 (96, 120, 144) sc. Join.
Break yarn and weave in the ends.

**Finishing**
Blocking your basket into shape will help smooth out some of the unevenness that is common when working with a stiff fiber like jute. If required, spritz with water and use a flat object such as a plate or tin to shape the bottom and plastic shopping bags to shape the top. Do be aware that the colored twines may bleed when wet.

# a place to perch

Make unexpected guests feel like they have the best seat in the house with these lovely chair pads (even if they are sitting on a spare stool)!

## skill level **beginner**

| Size | Rectangular | Large |
| --- | --- | --- |
| Finished width | 15¼ in | 17¼ in |
| Finished height | 10¼ in | 17¼ in |
| Yarn amount (Colour A) | 22 yd | 28 yd |
| Yarn amount (Colour B) | 252 yd | 361 yd |
| Yarn amount (Colour C) | 39 yd | 39 yd |
| Yarn amount (Colour D) | 128 yd | 50 yd |

Photos show rectangular size.

### materials:

* Color A: 1 x 1¾ oz ball of Drops Paris Cotton (100% cotton), Pistachio
* Color B: 5 (7) x 1¾ oz ball of Drops Paris Cotton (100% cotton), Off White
* Color C: 1 x 1¾ oz ball of Drops Paris Cotton (100% cotton), Light Purple
* Color D: 1 x 1¾ oz ball of Drops Paris Cotton (100% cotton), Light Ice Blue
* G/6 hook

### yarn review:

This hard-wearing sport weight cotton comes in an amazing range of colors so you can choose your own color scheme.

### yarn alternative:

Rico Design Essentials Cotton DK

### gauge:

1 small motif measures 5 in square.

### special stitch:

**Popcorn Stitch (PS)**

Make 5 dc into the next stitch, remove the hook from the loop and insert from front to back into the top of the first dc. Insert the hook into the loop that has been left and pull through the stitch. At the beginning of the round, the 3 chains count as the first dc.

### pattern note:

Popcorn stitches may need to be turned out with your fingers if they aren't popping out towards the front. The large size is an expanded version of the smaller motifs that make up the rectangular pad.

*The puffiness of these popcorn stitches makes a perfect chair pad.*

## rectangular chair pad instructions:

**Small Granny Squares (Make 6)**

**Rnd 1:** With Color A and working into magic loop (see Techniques, page 17), ch 3, [1PS, ch 5] four times. Join. Break yarn. 4 PS.

**Rnd 2:** Join Color B in ch5-space, ch 3, *(1PS, ch 5, 1PS) into ch5-space, ch 3, skip 1PS; rep from * around. Join. Break yarn. 8PS.

**Rnd 3:** Join Color C in 5ch-space, ch 3, *(1PS, ch 5, 1PS) into ch5-space, ch 3, skip 1PS, 1PS in ch3-space, skip 1PS; rep from * around. Join. Break yarn. 12 PS.

**Rnd 4:** Join Color B in ch5-space, ch 3, *(1PS, ch 5, 1PS) into ch5-space, ch 3, skip 1PS, [1PS in ch3-space, skip 1PS] twice; rep from * around. Join. Break yarn. 16 PS.

**Rnd 5:** Join Color D in ch5-space, ch 3, *(1PS, ch 5, 1PS) into ch5-space, ch 3, skip 1PS, [1PS in ch3-space, skip 1PS] three times; rep from * around. Join. Break yarn. 20 PS. Join the granny squares. Using Color D, hold two squares RS together. Work 3 sc into each ch-space, working through both squares to join. Using the photographs as a guide, join the granny squares in two rows of three.

### Back of Pad

Using Color B, ch 77 (86).

**Row 1:** Starting in 4th ch from hook (counts as 1 dc), 74 (83) dc. Turn. 75 (84) sts.

**Row 2:** Ch3 (counts as 1 dc), 74 (83) dc. Turn.

Work Row 2 until the piece measures 10¼ (17¼) in.

## large chair pad instructions:

Work Rnds 1–5 of a small granny square as for the rectangular chair pad.

**Rnd 6:** Join Color B in ch5-space, ch 3, *(1PS, ch 5, 1PS) into ch5-space, ch 3, skip 1PS, [1PS in ch3-space, skip 1PS] four times; rep from *around. Join. Break yarn. 24 PS.

**Rnd 7:** Join Color A in ch5-space, ch 3, *(1PS, ch 5, 1PS) into 5ch-space, ch 3, skip 1PS, [1PS in ch3-space, skip 1PS] five times; rep from * around. Join. Break yarn. 28 PS.

**Rnd 8:** Join Color B in ch5-space, ch 3, *(1PS, ch 5, 1PS) into ch5-space, ch 3, skip 1PS, [1PS in ch3-space, skip 1PS] six times; rep from * around. Join. Break yarn. 32 PS.

**Rnd 9:** Join Color C in ch5-space, ch 3, *(1PS, ch 5, 1PS) into ch5-space, ch 3, skip 1PS, [1PS in ch3-space, skip 1PS] seven times; rep from * around. Join. Break yarn. 36 PS.

**Rnd 10:** Join Color B in ch5-space, ch 3, *(1PS, ch 5, 1PS) into ch5-space, ch 3, skip 1PS, [1PS in ch3-space, skip 1PS] eight times; rep from * around. Join. Break yarn. 40 PS.

**Rnd 11:** Join Color D in ch5-space, ch 3, *(1PS, ch 5, 1PS) into ch5-space, ch 3, skip 1PS, [1PS in ch3-space, skip 1PS] nine times; rep from * around. Join. Break yarn. 44 PS.

### Back of Pad

Work as for the rectangular chair pad.

### Finishing Both Chair Pads

Place top and bottom pieces WS together. With the top facing, join Color D and dc around the edge, working into the ch-spaces on the top and the corresponding stitches or row ends on the bottom.

# table runner

This elegant table runner is made out of gorgeous, flower-inspired motifs.

## skill level **intermediate**

| Size | One size |
|------|----------|
| Width | 15¼ in |
| Length | 61½ in |
| Yarn amount | 722 yd |

**materials:**

* 2 x 3½ oz hanks of Fyberspates Shelia's Sock (75% superwash merino, 25% nylon), Oyster
* F/5 hook

**yarn review:**

This hand-dyed sock yarn adds subtle color changes and is supremely washable, making this a very usable table runner.

**yarn alternative:**

Artesano Definition Sock

**gauge:**

1 motif measures 5 in across using F/5 hook.

**special stitches:**

**Bobble Stitch (BS)**

[YO, insert the hook into the stitch, YO and pull through the stitch, YO and pull through two loops] three times, YO and pull through all the loops on your hook.

**Beginning Bobble Stitch (beg BS)**

[YO, insert the hook into the stitch, YO and pull through stitch, YO and pull through two loops] twice, YO and pull through all the loops on the hook.

**Cluster Decrease (cl dec)**

[YO, insert the hook into the BS, YO and pull through stitch, YO, pull through two loops] three times, YO, skip (ch 1, 1 dc, ch 1) and insert the hook into the top of the next BS, pull through stitch, YO, pull through two

loops, [YO, insert the hook into the stitch, YO and pull through stitch, YO, pull through two loops] three times, YO, pull through all seven loops on the hook.

**pattern note:**

You can omit the joining around and sew your motifs together if preferred.

## instructions (make 36):

Chain 5 and join into a loop with a sl st.

**Rnd 1:** Ch3 (counts as 1 dc in a BS), working into center of loop, 1beg BS, [ch 3, 1BS] five times, ch 3. Join into top of beg ch. [6BS].

**Rnd 2:** (Ch3 (counts as 1 dc in a BS), 1beg BS, 1BS) into BS, [ch 2, 1 dc into ch-space, ch 2, 2BS into BS] five times, ch 2, 1 dc into ch-space, ch 2. Join into top of beg ch. [12 BS and 6 dc sts].

**Rnd 3:** 2 sl st to second BS, ch 3, (counts as 1 dc in a BS), 1 beg BS, [ch 3, skip ch 2, 1 dc in dc, ch 3, skip ch 2, 1BS, 4ch, 1BS] five times, ch 3, skip ch 2, 1 dc in dc, ch 3, skip ch 2, 1BS into sl st at start of round, 4ch. Join.

**Rnd 4:** Ch3 (counts as 1 dc in a BS), 1beg BS, [ch 1, 1 dc into dc, ch 1, 1BS into BS, ch 5, 1 sc into ch-space, ch 5, 1BS into BS] five times, ch 5, 1 sc into ch-space, ch 5. Join.

**Rnd 5:** Ch3 (does not count as a st), [1cl dec, ch 7, 1 sc into ch-space, skip 1 sc, ch 5, 1 sc into ch-space, 6ch] six times. Join.

### Joining Round

When joining adjacent motifs, work the bracketed section of Rnd 5 as follows with Motif A being the motif you are currently working on and Motif B the motif you are joining onto: [1cl dec, ch 3, 1 sc into the adjacent ch5-space of Motif B, ch 3, 1 sc into ch-space of Motif A, skip 1 sc, ch 2, 1 sc into ch5-space of Motif B, 2 sc, 1 sc into next ch-space of Motif A, ch 3, 1 sc into adjacent ch5-space of Motif B, ch 3]. Repeat as required around Motif A to join adjacent motifs.

Follow the diagram for the motif layout.

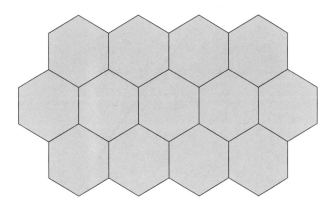

*This would make a gorgeous host gift, paired with a bottle of wine or a bouquet of wild flowers.*

# zigzag hottie

This classic blanket pattern is transformed into a snuggly cover for a hot water bottle.

## skill level **beginner**

| Size | 2-pint hottie | 4-pint hottie |
|---|---|---|
| Circumference | 13 in | 17 in |
| Length | 8¼ in | 10½ in |
| Yarn amount (Colors A and B) | 44 yd | 55 yd |
| Yarn amount (Color C) | 22 yd | 22 td |

Photos show 4-pint hot water bottle.

**materials:**

* Color A: 1 (1) x 1½ oz ball of King Cole Merino Blend Chunky (100% wool), Saxe
* Color B: 1 (1) x 1½ oz ball of King Cole Merino Blend Chunky (100% wool), White
* Color C: 1 (1) x 1½ oz ball of King Cole Merino Blend Chunky (100% wool), Scarlet
* J/10 hook
* Safety pins
* 2-pint (4-pint) hot water bottle

**yarn review:**

This 100% merino superwash bulky wool is gorgeously soft and very washable, making it perfect for a hot water bottle cover.

**yarn alternative:**

Wendy Merino Chunky

**gauge:**

Work 10 sts and 10 rows in single crochet in BLO to measure 4 in square using J/10 hook, or size needed to achieve gauge.

**pattern notes:**

Carry the yarn up the side of your work as you change colors to minimize the number of ends you have to weave in.
Do not count the t-ch as a stitch.

*Made with chunky wool, this is the perfect last-minute 'Get Well Soon' gift.*

## instructions:

With Color A, ch 40 (53).

**Row 1 (WS):** Starting in second ch from hook, 1 sc, skip 1 ch, 4 sc, *3 sc in next ch, 5 sc, skip 2 ch, 5 sc; rep from * until 7 ch from end, 3 sc in next ch, 4 sc, skip 1 ch, 1 sc. Turn. 39 (52) sts.

**Rows 2–4 (working in BLO):** Ch 1, 1 sc, skip 1 st, 4 sc, *3 sc in next st, 5 sc, skip 2 sts, 5 sc; rep from * until 7 sts from end, 3 sc in next st, 4 sc, skip 1 st, 1 sc. Turn.

**Rows 5–8 (working in BLO):** With Color B, ch 1, 1 sc, skip 1 st, 4 sc, *3 sc in next, 5 sc, skip 2 sts, 5 sc; rep from * until 7 sts from end, 3 sc in next st, 4 sc, skip 1 st, 1 sc. Turn.

**Rows 9–12 (working in BLO):** With Color A, ch 1, 1 sc, skip 1 st, 4 sc, *3 sc in next st, 5 sc, skip 2 sts, 5 sc; rep from * until 7 sts from end, 3 sc in next st, 4 sc, skip 1 st, 1 sc. Turn. Work Rows 5–12 a total of 5 (6) times. For the large hottie, work Rows 5–8 once more.

### Edging Row

Switch to Color C; repeat Row 2.

### Sewing Up Bottom Cover

With WS facing, fold the cover so that the edging row will run vertically up the center of the hot water bottle, with the ends overlapping by approximately 1½ in. Pin in place. Turn the cover inside out and, working into the row ends, sl st one end closed. Sl st both ends of what will be the neck edge of the cover when closed, leaving a 2¾ in gap in the middle.

### Neck Ribbing

Rejoin Color C at the neck edge of the cover; ch 21.

**Row 1:** Starting in second ch from hook, 20sc. 1sl st into next 3 sts on neck edge of cover. Turn. 20 sts.

**Row 2:** 20sc in BLO. Turn.

**Row 3:** Ch 1, 20sc in BLO, 1sl st into next 3 sts on neck edge of cover. Turn.

Repeat Rows 2–3 until all stitches around the neck of the cover are worked. When working into the overlapped section at the front of the cover, work through both layers of the cover.

Break yarn and weave in ends.

# For Her

*******

# best bib and tucker necklace

Worked in a small amount of luxury yarn with delicate pearls, this vintage-feel necklace is quick and easy to work up.

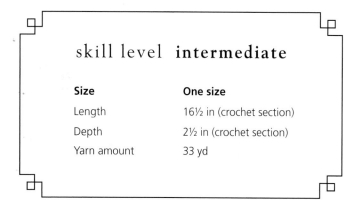

### skill level **intermediate**

| Size | One size |
|------|----------|
| Length | 16½ in (crochet section) |
| Depth | 2½ in (crochet section) |
| Yarn amount | 33 yd |

## materials:

* 1 x 1¾ oz cone of Jaipur Fino Silk (100% mulberry silk), Cream
* B/1 hook
* 3 seed pearls
* Length of thread (for loading pearls onto the yarn)
* A chain bracelet with clasps attached
* Pliers, strong scissors or tin snips

## yarn review:

This 100% silk lace-weight yarn is simply glamorous.

## yarn alternative:

DMC Petra Cotton Perle No 3 Crochet Cotton

## gauge:

The work measures 16½ in x ½ in at the end of Row 2.

## pattern note:

Unless otherwise stated, do not work into stitches; work only into chains.

## instructions:

Ch 147.

**Row 1:** Starting in second ch from hook, 1 sc *ch 4, skip 4ch, 1 sc in next ch; rep from * to end. 30 sc.

**Row 2 (RS):** Ch 1, [(2 sc, 2hdc, 2 sc) in ch4-space] eight times, [(2 sc, 1hdc, ch 4, 1hdc, 2 sc) in ch4-space] 13 times, [(2 sc, 2hdc, 2 sc) in ch4-space] eight times, 1 sc in tch, rotate to work into other side (fch), [6 sc into ch4-space] 29 times, sl st into sc. Break yarn. 349 sts.

**Row 3:** Load pearls onto yarn for later use. With RS facing reattach yarn to first ch4-space created in Row 2, (ch 3 (counts as 1 dc), 4 dc, ch 2, 5 dc) into ch4-space [(5 dc, ch 2, 5 dc)

into next ch4-space] 12 times. Turn. 130 sts.

**Row 4 (WS):** Sl st to ch2-space, 1 sc in ch-space, [(3tr, ch 1, 3tr, ch 1, 3tr) in next ch-space, 1 sc in next ch-space] six times. Turn. 61 sts.

**Row 5:** Sl st to ch-space, 1 sc in ch-space, ch 5, 3 dc in next ch-space, ch 1, [(3 dc, ch 1, 3 dc, ch 1) in next ch-space] eight times, 3 dc in next ch-space, ch 5, 1 sc in next ch-space. Turn. 56 sts.

**Row 6:** 3 sc in ch-space, ch 5, [skip ch1-space, 3 dc in next ch-space, ch 1, 5tr in next ch-space, ch 1, 3 dc in next ch-space, ch 1] four times, ch 4, 1 sc in next ch-space. Turn. 48 sts.

**Row 7:** 3 sc in ch-space, 5 dc in next ch-

space, ch 2, [9 dc in next ch-space, 1 sc in next ch-space, 9 dc in next ch sp, ch 2] three times, ch 2, 5 dc in next ch-space, 1 sc in next ch-space. Turn. 71 sts.

**Row 8:** Sl st to ch-space, [2 sc in ch-space, ch 6, 1tr in sc, place bead next to hook, ch 1 to secure bead in place, 1tr in same sc, 6ch] three times, 2 sc in next ch-space. Break yarn and fasten off. 14 sts.

### Finishing

Wet block to open the lace pattern. Weave in ends. Use tin snips, pliers or scissors to remove a link from center of bracelet. Sew bracelet halves securely to ends of Row 2.

*Combining different threads and beads will change the look and feel of this gorgeous gift.*

# shell scape

Normally, I'm not a fan of projects that are made in lots of parts (all those ends!), but this gorgeous shawl is worth the extra effort.

## skill level **intermediate**

| Size | One size |
|---|---|
| Finished wingspan | 42½ in |
| Finished depth from neck to hem | 19¾ in |
| Yarn amount | 668 yd |

**materials:**
* 3 x 3½ oz hanks of Ripples Craft Merino Sport (100% superwash merino), Assynt Lochs
* J/10 hook

**yarn review:**
I can't say enough good things about this gorgeous, sport-weight superwash wool. It crochets up like a dream, with excellent stitch definition and drape.

**yarn alternatives:**
Cascade 220 Superwash Sport
MillaMia Naturally Soft Merino

**gauge:**
1 shell motif measures 4 in high x 4¾ in wide at the base using J/10 hook or size required to obtain gauge.

**special stitches:**
**Puff Stitch (PS)**
[YO, insert the hook into the stitch and draw up a loop] five times (11 loops on the hook). YO and pull through all loops on the hook.

**Single Crochet 3 Together (sc3tog)**
[Insert the hook into the next stitch, YO and draw up a loop] three times (4 loops on the hook). YO and pull through all loops on the hook.

**pattern notes:**
Motifs are joined as you go. Making each motif requires breaking the yarn at the top point. To minimize having to weave in ends, make sure to crochet over the loose ends (see Techniques, page 18).
When working the joining sc up the row ends of the previous motif, exact placement of the stitches isn't crucial. Simply ensure they are evenly spaced up the row ends.
Do not count tch as a stitch unless specified.

## instructions:

**Basic Motif**

Make 21fsc. Turn.

**Row 1 (WS):** Ch 1, [1 sc, ch 1, skip 1fsc] ten times, 1 sc. Turn. 11 sts.

**Row 2:** Ch 1, 1 sc, [ch 1, 1PS in ch-space, skip 1 sc] ten times, 1 sc. Turn. 12 sts.

**Row 3:** Ch 1, 1 sc, [skip 1PS, 1 sc in ch-space] nine times, skip 1PS and ch 1, 1 sc. Turn. 11 sts.

**Row 4:** 4ch (counts as 1 dc and ch 1), skip 1 sc, [1 dc, ch 1, skip 1 sc] four times, 1 dc. Turn. 6 sts.

**Row 5:** Ch 1, [1 sc in dc, ch 1, skip 1 dc] five times, 1 sc in tch. Turn. 6 sts.

**Row 6:** Ch 1, 1 sc in sc, [1PS in ch-space, ch 1, skip 1 sc] five times, 1 sc. Turn. 7 sts.

**Row 7:** Ch 1, skip 1 sc and 1PS [1 sc in ch-space, skip 1PS] five times, 1 sc. Turn. 6 sts.

**Row 8:** Ch 1, 1 sc2tog, 1 sc, 1 sc 2 tog. Turn. 3sts.

**Row 9:** Ch 1, 3 sc. Turn.

**Row 10:** Ch 1, 1 sc3tog. Fasten off and break yarn.

**Motif Right Edge (MR)**

**Set-up row:** Make 11fsc, RS facing. Working evenly into row ends of previous motif 10sc from bottom edge to tip. Turn. 21 sts. Work Rows 1–10 of the basic motif pattern.

**Middle Motif (MM)**

**Set-up row:** Join yarn to tip of motif, 10sc from tip of motif down to bottom edge, 11 sc on next motif from bottom edge up to tip. Turn. 21 sts. Work Rows 1–10 of the basic motif pattern.

*Made in white or cream, this would make a beautiful wedding shawl.*

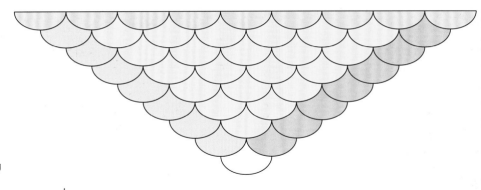

## Motif Left Edge (ML)

**Set-up row:** Working evenly into row ends of previous motif, 10sc from tip of motif down to bottom edge, ch 2 (this forms the basis of the 1st fdc), 11fsc. Turn. 21 sts.

Work Rows 1–10 of the basic motif pattern.

## Half Motif Right (HMR)

**Set-up row:** Make 11fsc, RS facing. Working evenly into row ends of previous motif 10sc from bottom edge to tip. Turn. 21 sts.

**Row 1 (WS):** Ch 1, [1 sc, ch 1, skip 1fsc] ten times, 1 sc. Turn. 11 sts.

**Row 2:** Ch 1, 1 sc, [ch 1, 1PS in ch-space, skip 1 sc] ten times, 1 sc. Turn. 12 sts.

**Row 3:** Ch 1, 1 dc, [miss 1PS, 1 dc in ch-space] nine times, miss 1PS and 1ch, 1 dc. Turn. 11 sts.

**Row 4:** Ch 1, 5 dc2tog, 1 dc. Turn. 6 sts.

**Row 5:** Ch 1, 3 dc2tog. Break yarn. 3 sts.

## Half Motif Middle (HMM)

**Set-up row:** Join yarn to tip of motif, 10sc from tip of motif down to bottom edge, 11 sc on next motif from bottom edge up to tip. Turn. 21 sts.

**Row 1 (WS):** Ch 1, [1 sc, ch 1, skip 1fsc] ten times, 1 sc. Turn. 11 sts.

**Row 2:** Ch 1, 1 sc, [ch 1, 1PS in ch-space, skip 1 sc] ten times, 1 sc. Turn. 12 sts.

**Row 3:** Ch 1, 1 sc, [skip 1PS, 1 sc in ch-space] nine times, skip 1PS and ch 1, 1 sc. Turn. 11 sts.

**Row 4:** Ch 1, 5 sc2tog, 1 sc. Turn. 6 sts.

**Row 5:** Ch 1, 3 sc2tog. Break yarn. 3 sts.

## Half Motif Left (HML)

**Set-up row:** Working evenly into row ends

 *Motif Right Edge (MR)*

 *Motif Left Edge (ML)*

 *Middle Motif (MM)*

 *Half Motif Right/*
*Half Motif Middle/*
*Half Motif Left*

of previous motif, 10sc from tip of motif down to bottom edge, ch 2 (this forms basis of 1st fsc), 11fsc. Turn. 21 sts.

**Row 1 (WS):** Ch 1, [1 sc, ch 1, skip 1fsc] ten times, 1 sc. Turn. 11 sts.

**Row 2:** Ch 1, 1 sc, [ch 1, 1PS in ch-space, miss 1 sc] ten times, 1 sc. Turn. 12 sts.

**Row 3:** Ch 1, 1 sc, [skip 1PS, 1 sc in ch-space] nine times, skip 1PS and ch 1, 1 sc. Turn. 11 sts.

**Row 4:** Ch 1, 5 sc2tog, 1 sc. Turn. 6 sts.

**Row 5:** Ch 1, 3 sc2tog. Break yarn. 3 sts.

## Construction

See the schematic for visual instructions on construction.

**Row 1:** Make 1 Basic Motif.

**Row 2:** 1MR, 1ML.

**Row 3:** 1MR, 1MM, 1ML.

**Row 4:** 1MR, 2MM, 1ML.

**Row 5:** 1MR, 3MM, 1ML.

**Row 6:** 1MR, 4MM, 1ML.

**Row 7:** 1MR, 5MM, 1ML.

**Row 8:** 1MR, 6MM, 1ML.

**Row 9:** 1HMR, 7HMM, 1HML.

## Edging

Rejoin the yarn on top of the straight edge, RS facing. Sc evenly across. Break yarn.

## Finishing

Weave in and trim any remaining ends. Block to the finished measurements.

# slouch and bobble hat

This is the perfect hat for hitting the slopes or the shops.

## skill level **advanced beginner**

| Size | Small | Medium | Large |
|---|---|---|---|
| Brim circumference | 20½ in | 21¼ in | 22½ in |
| Height | 10¼ in | 10½ in | 11 in |
| Yarn amount (MC) | 153 yd | 159 yd | 186 yd |
| Yarn amount (CC) | 120 yd | 126 yd | 131 yd |

**materials:**

* Main Color (MC): 1 x 3½ oz hank of
  Quince and Co Osprey (100% wool),
  Bird's Egg
* Contrast Color (CC): 1 x 3½ oz hank of
  Quince and Co Osprey (100% wool),
  Honey
* H/8 hook

**yarn review:**

This worsted-weight yarn has a smooth
handle and comes in a rainbow of colors.

**yarn alternative:**

Cascade 220

**gauge:**

Work 14 sts and 4.5 rows in Post Stitch
Ribbing to measure 4 in square using H/8
hook, or size needed to achieve gauge.

**pattern notes:**

Do not count the tch as a stitch unless
stated.

*This is a fun pattern to play with color. Try keeping the ribbing and double crochet the same color and alternating color on the single crochet stitches for a different look.*

**Post Stitch Ribbing**

With MC, leaving a 6 in tail for sewing up the gap in the ribbing at the end, 72 (76, 80) fdc. Join to work in the round.

**Rnds 1–4:** Ch3, *1fpdc, 1bpdc; rep from * around. Join. 72 (76, 80) sts.

**Hat**

**Rnd 1:** Join CC, ch 1, *1 sc into fpdc, ch 2, skip 1bpdc rep, from * around. Join. 36 (38, 40) sts.

**Rnd 2:** With MC, 1sl st to ch-space, ch 3 (counts as 1 dc), 2 dc into ch-space, ch 1, skip 1 sc, *3 dc into ch-space, ch 1, skip 1 sc; rep from * around. Join. 108 (114, 120) sts.

**Rnd 3:** Switch to CC, ch 1, 1 sc into last ch-space of previous round, ch 2, skip 3 dc, *1 sc into ch-space, ch 2, skip 3 dc; rep from * around. Join.

Work Rows 2–3 a total of 8 (8, 9) times (for a less slouchy hat, work fewer repeats).

## Crown Decreases

**Rnd 1:** 1sl st to ch-space, ch 3 (counts as 1 dc), 1 dc into ch-space, ch 1, skip 1 sc, *2 dc into ch-space, ch 1, skip 1 sc; rep from * around. Join. 72 (76, 80) sts.

**Rnd 2:** Switch to CC, ch 1, 1 sc into last ch-space of the previous round, skip 2 dc, *1 sc into ch-space, skip 2 dc; rep from * around. Join. Break yarn. 36 (38, 40) sts.

## Finishing

Using the yarn and needle, sew up the gap at the top of the hat, pulling tight to gather the stitches together. Tie the yarn off to secure. Using the tail left at the beginning foundation round, sew up the gap at the bottom edge of the ribbing. Make a large pompom out of CC (see Techniques, page 21) and sew securely to the top of the hat.

# *thrummed mittens*

A layer of warm unspun wool makes these mittens the softest, cosiest things you have ever put on your hands.

## skill level **intermediate**

| Size | Baby | Child | Small | Medium | Large |
|---|---|---|---|---|---|
| Finished circumference | 6 in | 6¾ in | 7½ in | 8¼ in | 10 in |
| Finished length from top to wrist | 5¼ in | 6 in | 6½ in | 7 in | 7¾ in |
| Yarn amount (MC): | 109 yd | 153 yd | 186 yd | 230 yd | 285 yd |

This pattern is designed to be worn with 1 in positive ease.

## materials:

* Main Color (MC): 1x 3½ oz hank of Ripples Craft Superwash Merino Sport (100% merino), Assynt Rocks
* Optional: a small amount of Contrast Color (CC): Ripples Craft Superwash Merino Sport (100% merino), Assynt Lochs
* 1¾ oz Ripples Craft BFL Top (100% wool), Assynt Lochs
* #7 hook
* F/5 hook
* Stitch marker

## yarn review:

This lovely sport-weight superwash merino wool is silky and light with excellent stitch definition.

## yarn alternatives:

Brown Sheep Nature Spun Sport for the main body of the mittens
Cascade Magum for the wool tops

## gauge:

Work 19 sts and 19 rows in thrummed double crochet to measure 4 in square using #7 hook, or size needed to achieve gauge.

## special techniques:

### Making a Thrum

Separate your fiber into a long strip, approximately ½ in wide. Starting at one end, pull a tuft off, about 4 in long. Fold each of the ends into the middle and gently roll the middle of the thrum between your fingers to lightly felt the ends.

### Working in a Thrum

Insert the hook into the stitch. Place the middle of the thrum on the hook, folding it in half around the hook. Holding it aside with the same hand that you use to hold your hook, YO, and pull both the YO and the thrum through the stitch. Yarn over again and pull through the loops and the thrum on your hook.

Thrums are worked in every fourth stitch in every third row to create a diagonal pattern. Some judgment will be needed at the start of each thrumming round to ensure even placement.

*If you can't find wool tops, use a single ply aran or chunky wool yarn.*

## instructions:

This section is worked in the round, amigurumi style, with no raising of the rounds or turning. Use a stitch marker to keep track of your rounds.

Thrums are worked on Rows 2, 5, 8, 11, 14, 17, 20, 23, 26, 29, 32, 35, 38, 41, 44, 47. Starting with MC and the larger hook, using a magic loop (see Techniques, page 17), ch 2 and 8 sc into the loop.

### Top of Mitten

**Rnd 1:** *2 sc into sc; rep from * around. 16 sc sts.

**Rnd 2 (thrummed round):** *1 sc, 2 sc into next sc; rep from * around. 24 sc sts.

### For size Baby ONLY

**Rnd 3:** *11 sc, 2 sc in next sc; rep from * around. 26 (-, -, -, -) dc sts.

### For sizes Child, Small, Medium and Large ONLY

**Rnd 3:** *2 sc, 2 sc into next sc; rep from * around. - (32, 32, 32, 32) sc sts.

### For size Small ONLY

**Rnd 4:** *15 sc, 2 sc into next sc; rep from * around. - (-, 34 -, -) sc sts.

### For size Medium and Large ONLY

**Rnd 4:** *3 sc, 2 sc into next sc; rep from * around. - (- , -, 40, 40) sc sts.

### For size Large ONLY

**Rnd 5 (thrummed round):** *4 sc, 2 sc into next sc; rep from * around. - (-, -. -, -, 48) sc sts.

### Hand

**Rnds 1–20 (23, 25, 27, 30):** (Remember to thrum on Round 5 and every 3rd round.) Work even in pattern. 26 (32, 34, 40, 48) sc sts.

**Rnd 21 (24, 26, 28, 31):** 1 sc, ch 5 (5, 7, 7, 8), skip 5 (5, 7, 7, 8) sts, sc in each st around to end. 21 (27, 28, 33, 41) sc sts. Sc into each st and ch around for 5 (6, 9, 9, 10) rounds. 26 (32, 34, 40, 48) sc sts.

### Cuff

**Rnds 1–8 (11, 11, 13, 13):** With smaller hook, ch 2 (does not count as a st), *1fpdc, 1bpdc; rep from * around. Do not turn. Join. 28 (32, 36, 40, 48) sts.

**Rnd 9 (12, 12, 14, 14):** If you are working a CC round, switch to CC, ch 1, 28 (32, 36, 40, 48) sts. Join. Break yarn.

### Thumb

This section is worked in the round,

amigurumi style, with no raising of the rounds or turning. Use a stitch marker to keep track of your rounds.

Rejoin MC at the first missed stitch for the thumbhole. 12 (12, 16, 16, 20) sc around the thumbhole, working across the skipped stitches and the chains and into the row ends at each side of the opening. 12 (12, 16, 16, 20) sts.

**Rnds 1–7 (8, 9, 10, 11):** 12 (12, 16, 16, 20) sc, (thrum rounds 3,6, and 9 as required), 12 (12, 16, 16, 20) sts.

**Rnd 8 (9, 10, 11, 12):** *1 sc2tog, 2 sc; rep from * around. 9 (9, 12, 12, 15) sts.

**Rnd 9 (10, 11, 12, 13):** *1 sc2tog, 1 sc; rep from * around. 6 (6, 8, 8, 10) sts.

**Rnd 10 (11, 12, 13, 14):** 1 sc2tog around. 3 (3, 4, 4, 5) sts.

### Finishing

Sew in ends.

# buttoned capelet

Worn on its own or under a jacket as a cowl,
this is a very versatile garment.

## skill level **intermediate**

| Size | Small | Medium | Large | Extra large |
|---|---|---|---|---|
| Finished circumference at bottom hem | 51½ in | 59¾ in | 67¾ in | 75½ in |
| Finished length from first buttonhole to hem | 16½ in | 17¼ in | 18 in | 19 in |
| Yarn amount | 826 yd | 996 yd | 1177 yd | 1376 yd |

### materials:
* 3 (3, 3, 4) x 4 oz hanks of 4-ply Fyberspates Vivacious (100% merino), Deep Forest
* 3 (3, 3, 4) x buttons, approximately 1 in diameter
* #7 hook

### yarn review:
This slightly variegated sock yarn is very washable and durable.

### yarn alternative:
Rowan Fine Nordic Tweed

### gauge:
Work 19 stitches and 11 rows in linked treble crochet to measure 4 in square using #7 hook, or size required to achieve gauge.

### special stitches:
**Linked Double Crochet (ldc)**
First Stitch after tch:
Insert the hook into the second chain of the turning chain, YO and pull through, insert the hook into the next stitch, YO and pull through, YO, pull the loop through the two loops on the hook, YO, pull through the last two loops.

All other stitches:
Insert the hook into the middle loop of the stitch just worked, YO and pull through, insert the hook into the next stitch, YO and pull through, YO, pull the loop through the two loops on the hook, YO, pull through the last two loops.

**Back Post Single Crochet (BPsc)**
Insert the hook from the back of the fabric around the front of the post of the stitch below and then out the back of the fabric, YO and pull through the stitch, YO and pull through the two loops on the hook.

### pattern note:
Count the turning chain as a stitch.

*The linked double crochet stitches give this capelet a lot of drape.*

**instructions:**
Ch82 (82, 101, 101).

### Neck Opening

**Row 1 (RS):** Starting in 4th ch from the hook (counts as 1 dc), 78 (78, 97, 97) ldc. Turn. 79 (79, 98, 98) sts.

**Rows 2–17:** Ch3, 78 (78, 97, 97) ldc. Turn.

### Shoulder to Ripple

**Row 1 (RS):** Ch3, 1ldc, ch 1, skip 1ldc, [2ldc in next ldc, 3 (3, 4, 4) ldc] 19 times. Turn. 97 (97, 116, 116) sts.

**Row 2 and all WS rows:** Ldc into each ldc and ch across.

**Row 3:** Ch3, 2ldc, [4 (4, 5, 5) ldc, 2ldc in next ldc] 19 times. Turn. 117 (117, 136, 136) sts.

**Row 5:** Ch3, 2ldc, [2ldc in next ldc, 5 (5, 6, 6)

ldc] 19 times. Turn. 136 (136, 155, 155) sts.

**Row 7:** Ch3, 2ldc, [6 (6, 7, 7) ldc, 2ldc in next ldc] 19 times. Turn. 155 (155, 174, 174) sts.

**Row 9 (buttonhole row):** Ch3, 1ldc, ch 1, skip 1ldc, [2ldc in next ldc, 7 (7, 8, 8) ldc] 19 times. Turn. 173 (173, 192, 192) sts.

**Row 11:** Ch3, 2ldc, [8 (8, 9, 9) ldc, 2ldc in next ldc] 19 times. Turn. 193 (193, 212, 212) sts.

**Row 13:** Ch3, 2ldc, [2ldc in next ldc, 9 (9, 10, 10) ldc] 19 times. Turn. 212 (212, 231, 231) sts.

**Row 15:** Ch3, 2ldc, [10 (10, 11, 11) ldc, 2ldc in next ldc] 19 times. Turn. 231 (231, 250, 250) sts.

**Row 17 (buttonhole row):** Ch3, 1ldc, ch 1, skip 1ldc, [2ldc in next ldc, 11 (11, 12, 12) ldc] 19 times. Turn. 249 (249, 268, 268) sts.

**For sizes Medium, Large and Extra Large ONLY**

**Row 19:** Ch3, 2ldc, [- (12, 13, 13) ldc, 2ldc in next ldc] 19 times. Turn. - (269, 288, 288) sts.

**Row 21:** Ch3, 2ldc, [2ldc in next ldc, - (13, 14, 14) ldc] 19 times. Turn. - (288, 307, 307) sts.

**For sizes Large and Extra Large ONLY**

**Row 23:** Ch3, 2ldc, [- (-, 15, 15) ldc, 2ldc in next ldc] 19 times. Turn. - (-, 326, 326) sts.

**For size Extra Large ONLY**

**Row 25 (buttonhole row):** Ch3, 1ldc, ch 1, skip 1ldc, [2ldc in next ldc, 16 ldc] 19 times. Turn. - (-, -, 345) sts.

**Row 27:** Ch3, 2ldc, [17ldc, 2ldc in next ldc] 19 times. Turn. - (-, -, 364) sts.

**ALL Sizes**

Work even for 3 (1, 1, -) rows.

**Joining for Working in the Rnd (ALL Sizes):**

Ch3, place the last 2 sts of the row under the first 3 sts in the row, 3ldc, working through both layers, 244 (282, 320, 358) ldc. Join. Do not turn. 247 (285, 323, 361) sts.

**Ripple**

Ripple notes:

Do not count the beginning chain as a stitch throughout this section.

Work in rounds with RS facing. Do not turn.

**Rnd 1 (RS) and all odd rows:** Ch1, 247 (285, 323, 361) BPsc. Join.

**Rnd 2:** Ch3, [5dc in next st, (1dc in next st, skip 1 st) eight times, 1dc, 5dc in next st] 13 (15, 17, 19) times. Join.

**Rnd 4:** Ch4, [5tr in next st, (1tr in next st, skip 1 st) eight times, 1tr, 5tr in next st] 13 (15, 17, 19) times. Join. Do not turn.

**Rnd 6:** Ch5, [5 dtr in next st, (1 dtr in next st, skip 1 st) eight times, 1 dtr, 5 dtr in next st] 13 (15, 17, 19) times. Join. Do not turn.

**Rnd 8:** As Round 2.

**Rnd 10:** As Round 4.

**Rnd 12:** As Round 6.

**Rnd 14:** As Round 2.

**Rnd 16:** As Round 4.

**Rnd 18:** As Round 6.

**Rnd 19:** As Round 1.

**Finishing**

Weave in the ends. Using the buttonholes for placement, sew on the buttons.

# waterfall shrug

This oversized cardigan is perfect for wrapping up on a cold day. Its simple construction makes it a perfect first garment.

## skill level **beginner**

| Size | Extra small | Small | Medium | Large | Extra large |
|---|---|---|---|---|---|
| Finished width (a) | 49 in | 55 in | 61½ in | 67¾ in | 74 in |
| Finished length (b) | 15 in | 15 in | 19 in | 19 in | 23 in |
| Shoulder to shoulder (c) | 19¾ in | 23¼ in | 23¼ in | 23¼ in | 29½ in |
| Yarn amount | 668 yd | 744 yd | 1029 yd | 1128 yd | 1467 yd |

## materials:

✱ 13 (14, 19, 21, 27) x 1¾ oz hanks of Artesano Alpaca DK (100% alpaca) in Sweet Pea

✱ H/8 hook

## yarn review:

Light as air and gorgeously drapy, this 100% alpaca sport-weight wool is a joy to work with.

## yarn alternative:

Artesano Superwash DK

## gauge:

16 sts and 8 rows in treble crochet to 4 in square using H/8 hook or size needed to achieve gauge.

Gauge square of Crossed Shell Stitch (see Special Stitches) measures 4¾ in x 4 in blocked.

## special stitches:

**Crossed Shell Stitch (CS):**

**Instructions for Gauge Swatch:**

Chain 29. (Stitch chart on page 81.)

**Set-up row:** 3 dc in fifth ch from hook (t-ch counts as 1 dc and ch 1), skip 3ch, [1 sc, skip 5ch, 3 dc in next ch, ch 2, working back in to second ch skipped, 3 dc, skip 5ch from st just made] twice, 1 sc, skip ch 3, (3 dc, ch 1, 1tr) into ch. Turn. 2 completed CS sts and 1 half CS at either end.

**Row 1:** Ch 1 (doesn't count as stitch), 1 sc into dc, ch 3, skip 3 dc, 1 dc into sc, [ch 3, skip 3 dc, 1 sc into ch 2-sp, ch 3, skip 3 dc, 1 dc into dc] twice, ch 3, skip 3 dc, 1 sc into ch-sp. Turn.

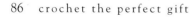

**Row 2:** Ch 1 (does not count as a st), 1 sc into sc, skip ch3-space and 1 dc, 3 dc into ch-space, [ch 2, 3 dc into skipped ch3-space, 1 sc into sc, skip ch 3-sp and 1 dc, 3 dc into ch3-space] twice, ch 2, 3 dc into skipped ch3-space, 1 sc into dc. Turn.

**Row 3:** Ch 6 (counts as 1 dc and ch 3), skip 3 dc, 1 sc into ch 2-sp, [ch 3, skip 3 dc, 1 dc into sc, skip 3 dc, 1 sc into ch 2-sp] twice, ch 3, skip 3 dc, 1 dc in sc. Turn.

**Row 4:** Ch 4 (counts as 1 dc and ch 3), 3 dc in dc, skip ch 3, [1 sc in sc, skip ch 3 and 1 dc, 3 dc into ch 3-sp, ch 2, 3 dc into skipped ch3-space] 4 times, 1 sc into sc, skip ch 3, (3 dc, ch 1, 1 dc) into ch. Turn.

Work Rows 1–4 a total of twice. Wash and block for gauge.

## pattern notes:

When crossing your stitches, work in front of the 3 dc group you have already made.

## instructions:

### Body:

Ch 261 (293, 325, 357, 389).

**Set-up row (RS):** 3 dc in fifth ch from hook (t-ch counts as 1 dc and ch 3), skip 3ch, [1 sc, skip 5ch, 3 dc in next ch, ch 2, working back into the second ch skipped, 3 dc, skip 5ch from the stitch just made] 31 (35, 39, 43, 47) times, 1 sc, skip 3ch, (3 dc, ch 1, 1 dc) into next ch. Turn. 31 (35, 39, 43, 47) CS sts.

**Row 1:** Ch 1 (does not count as a stitch), 1 sc into dc, ch 3, skip 3 dc, 1 dc into sc, [ch 3, skip 3 dc, 1 sc into ch2-space, ch 3, skip 3 dc, 1 dc into sc] 31 (35, 39, 43, 47) times, ch 3, skip 3 dc, 1 sc into ch-space. Turn. 32 (36, 40, 44, 48) dc sts.

**Row 2:** Ch 1 (does not count as a stitch), 1 sc into sc, skip ch 3-sp and 1 dc, 3 dc into ch-sp, [ch 2, 3 dc into skipped ch 3-sp, 1 sc into sc, skip ch 3-sp and 1 dc, 3 dc into ch 3-sp] 31 (35, 39, 43, 47) times, ch 2, 3 dc into skipped ch3-space, 1 sc into sc. Turn. 32 (36, 40, 44, 48) CS sts.

**Row 3:** Ch 6 (counts as 1 dc and ch 3), skip 3 dc, 1 sc into ch2-space, [ch 3, skip 3 dc, 1 dc into sc, skip 3 dc, 1 sc into ch2-space] 31 (35, 39, 43, 47) times, ch 3, skip 3 dc, 1 dc in sc. Turn. 33 (37, 41, 45, 49) dc sts.

**Row 4:** Ch 4 (counts as 1dc and ch 3), 3 dc in dc, skip ch 3 and 1 dc, [3 dc into ch 3-sp, ch 2, 3 dc into skipped ch 3-sp, 1 sc in sc, skip ch 3 and 1 dc] 31 (35, 39, 43, 47) times, 1 sc into sc skip ch 3, (3 dc, ch 1, 1 dc) into ch. Turn. 31 (35, 39, 43, 47) CS sts.

Work Rows 1–4 a total of 3 (3, 4, 4, 5) times. Work Rows 1–2 once more.

### Armholes:

**Armhole Row 1:** Ch 6 (counts as 1 dc and ch 3), skip 3 dc, 1 sc into ch2-space, [ch 3, skip 3 dc, 1 dc into sc, skip 3 dc, 1 sc into ch 2-sp] 8 (9, 10, 12, 12) times ch, 24 (32, 32, 32, 32), skip 2 (2, 3, 3, 3) CS, 1 sc into next ch2-space, [ch 3, skip 3 dc, 1 dc into sc, skip 3 dc, 1 sc into ch2-space] 12 (14, 14, 14) times ch, 24 (32, 32, 32, 32), skip 2 (2, 3, 3, 3) CS, 1 sc into next ch 2-sp, [ch 3, skip 3 dc, 1 dc into sc, skip 3 dc, 1 sc into ch 2-sp] 8 (9, 10, 12, 12) times, ch 3, skip 3 dc, 1 dc in sc. Turn.

**Armhole Row 2:** Ch 4 (counts as 1 dc and ch 3), 3 dc in dc, skip ch 3 and 1 dc, [3 dc into ch3-space, ch 2, 3 dc into skipped ch3-space, 1 sc in sc, skip ch 3 and 1 dc] 8 (9, 10, 12, 12) times, [1 sc into next ch, skip 5ch, 3 dc in next ch, ch 2, working back in to the second ch skipped, 3 dc, skip ch 1] 3 (3, 4, 4, 4) times, [1 sc in sc, skip ch 3 and 1 dc, 3 dc into ch 3-sp, ch 2, 3 dc into skipped ch 3-sp] 11 (13, 13, 13, 17) times, [1 sc into ch, skip 5ch, 3 dc in next ch, ch 2, working back in to second ch skipped, 3 dc, skip ch 1] 3 (4, 4, 4, 4) times, [1 sc in sc, skip ch 3 and 1 dc, 3 dc into ch 3-sp, ch 2, 3 dc into skipped ch 3-sp] 8 (9, 10, 12, 12) times, 1 sc into sc, [skip ch 3, (3 dc, ch 1, 1 dc) into ch. Turn. 31 (35, 39, 43, 47) CS sts.

Work body Rows 1–4 a total of 3 (3, 4, 4, 5) times.

Work Row 1 once more.

*The stitch pattern looks complicated at first, but after the set-up rows it is easily memorized.*

### Edging:

**Rnd 1:** Ch3, 258 (289, 321, 353, 385) dc, working into each stitch and chain across, (1 dc, ch 2, 1 dc) into corner stitch. Working into the row ends, 60 (60, 76, 76, 92) dc evenly spaced across, (1 dc, ch 2, 1 dc) into corner stitch. Working into the beg-ch, 256 (288, 320, 352, 384) dc, (1 dc, ch 2, 1 dc) into corner stitch. Working into the row ends, 60 (60, 76, 76, 92) dc evenly spaced across, (1 dc, ch 2, 1 dc) into corner stitch. Join. 640 (704, 800, 864, 960) sts.

Break yarn. Block rectangle to open up the lace.

### Sleeves (Make 2):

**Set-Up row:** With RS facing, reattach yarn at the dc at the edge of the armhole. Working into the skipped stitches of Armhole Row 1, [ch 3, skip 3 dc, 1 dc into sc, skip 3 dc, 1 sc into ch2-space] 3 (3, 4, 4, 4) times.

**Rnd 1:** Ch 3 (counts as 1 dc), working across the chain from Round 15, 24 (24, 32, 32, 32) dc, 1 dc into each st and ch of the sleeve set up. Join. 48 (48, 64, 64, 64) sts.

**Rnds 2–24 (25, 26, 27, 27):** Ch3 (counts as 1 dc), 47 (47, 63, 63, 63) dc. Join. 48 (48, 64, 64, 64) sts.

Break yarn. Weave in ends.

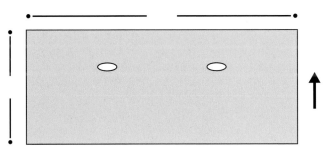

*abbreviated sample of stitch pattern*

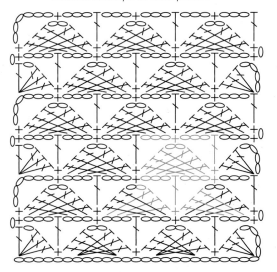

○ chain
┬ double crochet

┼ single crochet

# wedding bells

The perfect gift for a bride or bridal party, this pretty wrap will
do its best to prevent cold shoulders, if not cold feet!

## skill level **advanced**

| Size | Small | Medium | Large | Extra large |
|---|---|---|---|---|
| Finished bottom circumference | 39¾ in | 50 in | 59¾ in | 69¾ in |
| Finished length from neck to hem | 13½ in | 13½ in | 13½ in | 13½ in |
| Yarn amount | 514 yd | 646 yd | 772 yd | 987 yd |

Each size will fit a large range of chest sizes.

**materials:**

* 3 (4, 4, 5) x 1¾ oz hanks of 4-ply Artesano (100% alpaca), Cream
* #7 hook
* 24 in x 1 in wide ribbon

**yarn review:**

This fingering yarn is soft and elegant with the characteristic drape and slight halo of 100% alpaca.

**yarn alternative:**

Debbie Bliss Rialto
Artesano 4-ply

**gauge:**

Work 18 stitches and 11 rows in linked double crochet to measure 4 in square using #7 hook, or size needed to achieve gauge.

**special stitch:**

**Linked Double Crochet (ldc)**
**First Stitch after t-ch:**

Insert the hook into the second chain of the turning chain, YO and pull through, insert the hook into the next stitch, YO and pull through, YO, pull the loop through two loops on the hook, YO, pull through the last two loops.

**All other stitches:**

Insert the hook into the middle loop of the stitch just worked, YO and pull through, insert the hook into the next stitch, YO and pull through, YO, pull the loop through two loops on the hook, YO, pull through the last two loops.

## pattern notes:

Do not count the t-ch at the beginning of the rows as a stitch.

The shawl is worked in two parts out from either side of the beginning chain, which acts as the central back seam.

When working short rows, turn your work before the end of the row. As the rows get longer and you pass the step created by the previous short rows, work the first stitch as follows:

Insert the hook into the middle loop of the stitch just worked, YO and pull through, insert the hook into the second chain of t-ch one row below, YO and pull through, insert the hook through the middle bar of the stitch two rows below, YO and pull through, insert the hook into the next stitch, YO and pull through, YO and pull through four loops on the hook. YO and pull through all loops on the hook.

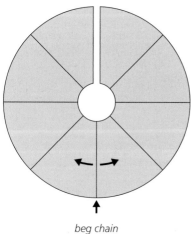

beg chain

*abbreviated sample of stitch pattern*

○  *chain*

ᵀ  *double crochet*

ᔈ  *post stitch double crochet*

i n s t r u c t i o n s :  Ch 77.

**Right Panel**

Row 1 (RS): Starting in fourth ch from hook, 3 dc in next ch, [skip 3ch, 2 dc, ch 1, skip 1ch, 2 dc, skip 3ch, (3 dc, ch 1, 3 dc) in next st] twice, skip 3ch, 2 dc, ch 1, skip 1ch, 2 dc, skip 3ch, 3 dc in next ch, ch 1, skip 1ch, 1 dc, 35ldc. Turn. 66 sts.

Row 2 (WS): Ch3, 35ldc, 1bpdc, ch 1, 3 dc in ch-space, [skip 3 dc, 2bpdc, ch 1, 2bpdc, skip 3 dc, (3 dc, ch 1, 3 dc) in ch-space] twice, skip 3 dc, 2 dc, ch 1, skip 1 dc, 2 dc, skip 3 dc, 3 dc in ch-space, 1 dc in tch. Turn. 67 sts.

Row 3: Ch4, 3dc in ch-space, [skip 3 dc, 2fpdc, ch 1, 2fpdc, skip 3 dc, (3 dc, ch 1, 3 dc) in ch-space] twice, skip 3 dc, 2 dc, ch 1, skip 1 dc, 2 dc, skip 3 dc, 3 dc in ch-space,

1fpdc. Turn. 31sts.

Row 4: Ch4, 2 dc, [skip 3 dc, 2bpdc, (1 dc, ch 1, 1 dc) in ch-space, 2bpdc, skip 3 dc, (2 dc, ch 1, 2 dc) in ch-space] twice, skip 3 dc, 2bpdc, (1 dc, ch 1, 1 dc) in ch-space, 2bpdc, skip 3 dc, 1 dc in ch-space, ch 1, 1 sc in tch. Turn 30 sts.

Row 5: Ch4, skip (1 dc, ch 1, 1 dc), 2fpdc, [skip 1 dc, (3 dc, ch 1, 3 dc) in ch-space, skip 1 dc, 2fpdc, ch 1, skip (2 dc, ch 1, 2 dc), 2fpdc] twice, skip 1 dc, (3 dc, ch 1, 3 dc) in ch-space, skip 1 dc, 2fpdc, ch 1, skip 2 dc, 1fpdc in tch, 7ldc. Turn. 38 sts.

Row 6: Ch3, 7ldc, 1bpdc, ch 1, 2bpdc, [skip 3 dc, (3 dc, ch 1, 3 dc) in ch-space, skip 3 dc, 2bpdc, ch 1, 2bpdc] twice, skip 3 dc, (3 dc, ch 1, 3 dc) in ch-space, skip 3 dc, 2bpdc, ch 1, 1 dc in tch. Turn. 39 sts.

Row 7: Ch4, 2fpdc, [skip 3 dc, (3 dc, ch 1, 3 dc) in ch-space, skip 3 dc, 2fpdc, ch 1, 2fpdc] twice, skip 3 dc, (3 dc, ch 1, 3 dc) in ch-space, skip 3 dc, 2fpdc, ch 1, 1fpdc, 14ldc. Turn. 46 sts.

Row 8: Ch3, 14ldc, 1bpdc, ch 1, 2bpdc, [skip 3 dc, (3 dc, ch 1, 3 dc) in ch-space, skip 3 dc, 2bpdc, ch 1, 2bpdc] twice, skip3 dc (3 dc, ch 1, 3 dc) in ch-space, skip 3 dc, 2bpdc, ch 1, 1 sc in tch. Turn.

Row 9: 4ch, 2fpdc, [skip 3 dc, (3 dc, ch 1, 3 dc) in ch-space, skip 3 dc, 2fpdc, ch 1, 2fpdc] twice, skip 3 dc, (3 dc, ch 1, 3 dc) in ch-space, skip 3 dc, 2fpdc, ch 1, 1fpdc, 21ldc. Turn. 52 sts.

Row 10: Ch3, 21ldc, 1bpdc, 1 dc in ch-space, 2bpdc, [skip 3 dc, (2 dc, ch 1, 2 dc) in ch-space, skip 3 dc, 2bpdc, (1 dc, ch 1, 1 dc)

in ch-space, 2bpdc] twice, skip 3 dc, (2 dc, ch 1, 2 dc) in ch-space, skip 3 dc, 2bpdc, 1 dc in ch-space, ch 1, skip 1fpdc, 1 dc in tch. Turn. 53 sts.

**Row 11:** Ch4 (counts as 1dc and ch 1), skip 1 dc, 3 dc in ch-space, [2fpdc, ch 1, skip (2 dc, ch 1, 2 dc), 2fpdc, skip 1 dc, (3 dc, ch 1, 3 dc) in ch-space] twice, 2fpdc, ch 1, skip (2 dc, ch 1, 2 dc), 2fpdc, skip 1 dc, 3 dc in ch-space, ch 1, 1fpdc, 35ldc. Turn. 66 sts.

**Row 12:** Ch3, 35ldc, 1bpdc, 3 dc in ch-space, [skip 3 dc, 2bpdc, ch 1, 2bpdc, skip 3 dc, (3 dc, ch 1, 3 dc) in ch-space] twice, skip 3 dc, 2bpdc, ch 1, skip 1bpdc, 2, skip 3 dc, 3 dc in ch-space, 1 dc in tch. Turn. 67 sts.

**Row 13:** Ch4, 3 dc, [skip 3 dc, 2fpdc, ch 1, 2fpdc, skip 3 dc, (3 dc, ch 1, 3 dc) in ch-space] twice, skip 3 dc, 2 dc, ch 1, skip 1 dc, 2 dc, skip 3 dc, 3 dc in ch-space, 1fpdc, 35ldc. Turn.

Work Rows 2–13 a total of 4 (5, 6, 7) times.

### Ribbon Hole Row

Ch3, 7ldc, ch 1, skip one st, 27ldc, 1bpdc, ch 1, 3 dc in ch-space, [skip 3 dc, 2bpdc, ch 1, 2bpdc, skip 3 dc, (3 dc, ch 1, 3 dc) in ch-space] twice, skip 3 dc, 2 dc, ch 1, skip 1 dc, 2 dc, skip 3 dc, 3 dc in ch-space, 1 dc in tch. Turn. Break yarn.

### Left Panel

**Row 1 (WS):** Rejoin yarn onto beg ch at cabled end, WS facing. Working into unworked side of beg ch, ch 4, 3 dc in next st, [skip 3 dc, 2 dc, ch 1, skip 1 dc, 2 dc, skip 3 dc, (3 dc, ch 1, 3 dc) in next st] twice, skip 3 dc, 2 dc, ch 1, skip 1 dc, 2 dc, skip 3 dc,

3 dc in next st, ch 1, skip 1 st, 1 dc, 35ldc. Turn. 66 sts.

**Row 2 (RS):** Ch3, 35ldc, 1fpdc, ch 1, 3 dc in ch-space, [skip 3 dc, 2fpdc, ch 1, 2fpdc, skip 3 dc, (3 dc, ch 1, 3 dc) in ch-space] twice, skip 3 dc, 2 dc, ch 1, skip 1 dc, 2 dc, skip 3 dc, 3 dc in ch-space, 1 dc in tch. Turn. 67 sts.

**Row 3:** Ch4, 3 dc in ch-space, [skip 3 dc, 2bpdc, ch 1, 2bpdc, skip 3 dc, (3 dc, ch 1, 3 dc) in ch-space] twice, skip 3 dc, 2 dc, ch 1, skip 1 dc, 2 dc, skip 3 dc, 3 dc in ch-space, 1bpdc. Turn. 31sts.

**Row 4:** Ch4, 2 dc in ch-space, [skip 3 dc, 2fpdc, (1 dc, ch 1, 1 dc) in ch-space, 2fpdc, skip 3 dc, (2 dc, ch 1, 2 dc) in ch-space] twice, skip 3 dc, 2fpdc, (1 dc, ch 1, 1dc) in ch-space, 2fpdc, skip 3 dc, 1 dc in ch-space, ch 1, 1 dc in tch. 30 sts.

**Row 5:** Ch4, skip (1 dc, ch 1, 1dc), 2bpdc, [skip 1 dc, (3 dc, ch 1, 3 dc) in ch-space, skip 1 dc, 2bpdc, ch 1, skip (2 dc, ch 1, 2 dc), 2bpdc] twice, skip 1 dc, (3 dc, ch 1, 3 dc) in ch-space, skip 1 dc, 2bpdc, ch 1, skip 2 dc, 1bpdc, 7ldc. Turn. 38 sts.

**Row 6:** Ch3, 7ldc, 1fpdc, ch 1, 2fpdc, [skip 3 dc, (3 dc, ch 1, 3 dc) in ch-space, skip 3 dc, 2fpdc, ch 1, 2fpdc] twice, skip 3 dc, (3 dc, ch 1, 3 dc) in ch-space, skip 3 dc, 2bpdc, ch 1, 1 dc in tch. Turn. 39 sts.

**Row 7:** Ch4, 2bpdc, [skip 3 dc, (3 dc, ch 1, 3dc) in ch-space, skip 3 dc, 2bpdc, ch 1, 2bpdc] twice, skip 3 dc, (3 dc, ch 1, 3 dc) in ch-space, skip 3 dc, 2bpdc, ch 1, 1bpdc, 14ldc. Turn. 45 sts.

**Row 8:** Ch3, 14ldc, 1fpdc, ch 1, 2fpdc, [skip 3 dc, (3 dc, ch 1, 3 dc) in ch-space, skip 3 dc, 2fpdc, ch 1, 2fpdc] twice, skip 3 dc, (3 dc, ch

1, 3 dc) in ch-space, skip 3 dc, 2bpdc, ch 1, 1 dc in tch. Turn.

**Row 9:** Ch4, 2bpdc [skip 3 dc, (3 dc, ch 1, 3 dc) in ch-space, skip 3 dc, 2bpdc, ch 1, 2bpdc] twice, skip 3 dc, (3 dc, ch 1, 3 dc) in ch-space, skip 3 dc, 2bpdc, ch 1, 1bpdc, 21ldc. Turn. 52 sts.

**Row 10:** Ch3, 21ldc, 1fpdc, 1 dc in ch-space, 2fpdc, [skip 3 dc, (2 dc, ch 1, 2 dc) in ch-space, skip 3 dc, 2fpdc, (1 dc, ch 1, 1 dc) in ch-space, 2fpdc] twice, skip 3 dc, (2 dc, ch 1, 2 dc) in ch-space, skip 3 dc, 2fpdc, 1 dc in ch-space, ch 1, 1 dc in tch. Turn. 53 sts.

**Row 11:** Ch4, 3 dc in ch-space, [2bpdc, ch 1, skip (2 dc, ch 1, 2 dc), 2bpdc, skip 1 dc, (3 dc, ch 1, 3 dc) in ch-space] twice, 2bpdc, ch 1, skip (2 dc, ch 1, 2 dc), 2bpdc, skip 1 dc, 3 dc in ch-space, ch 1, 1bpdc, 35ldc. Turn. 66 sts.

**Row 12:** Ch3, 35ldc, 1fpdc, 3 dc in ch-space, [skip 3 dc, 2fpdc, ch 1, 2fpdc, skip 3 dc, (3 dc, ch 1, 3 dc) in ch-space] twice, skip 3 dc, 2 dc, ch 1, skip 1 dc, 2 dc, skip 3 dc, 3 dc in ch-space, 1 dc in tch. Turn. 67 sts.

**Row 13:** Ch4, 3 dc in ch-space, [skip 3 dc, 2bpdc, ch 1, 2bpdc, skip 3 dc, (3 dc, ch 1, 3 dc) in ch-space] twice, skip 3 dc, 2 dc, ch 1, skip 1 dc, 2 dc, skip 3 dc, 3 dc in ch-space, 1bpdc, 35ldc. Turn.

Work Rows 2–13 a total of 4 (5, 6, 7) times.

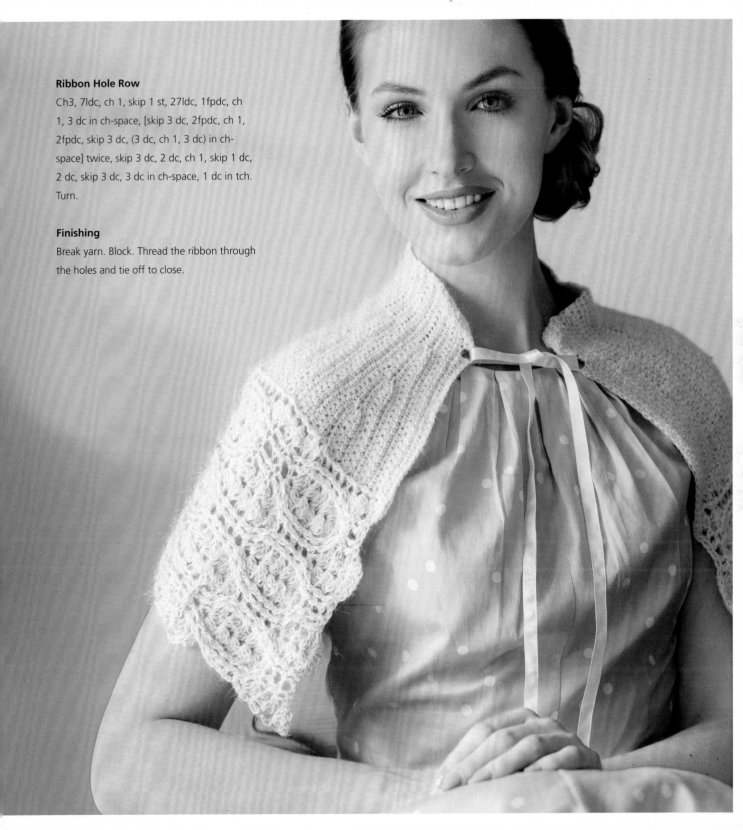

**Ribbon Hole Row**

Ch3, 7ldc, ch 1, skip 1 st, 27ldc, 1fpdc, ch 1, 3 dc in ch-space, [skip 3 dc, 2fpdc, ch 1, 2fpdc, skip 3 dc, (3 dc, ch 1, 3 dc) in ch-space] twice, skip 3 dc, 2 dc, ch 1, skip 1 dc, 2 dc, skip 3 dc, 3 dc in ch-space, 1 dc in tch. Turn.

**Finishing**

Break yarn. Block. Thread the ribbon through the holes and tie off to close.

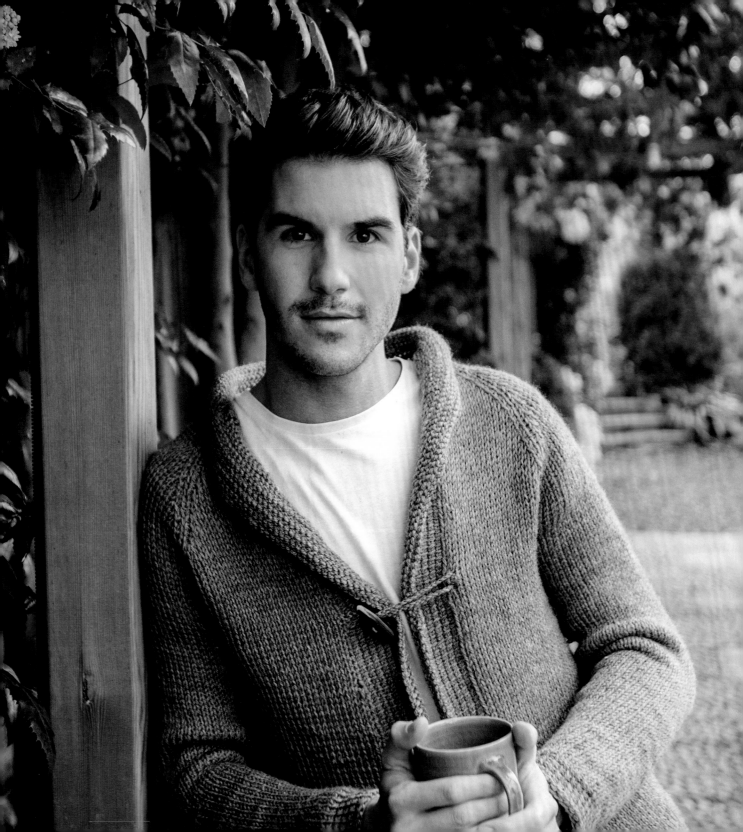

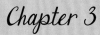

# For Him

✳ ✳ ✳ ✳ ✳ ✳ ✳

# knitterly hat

A simple change to a basic half double crochet creates a gender-neutral fabric, with a "knit look" stitch.

## skill level **beginner**

| Size | Newborn | Baby | Toddler | Child | Adult |
|---|---|---|---|---|---|
| Finished brim circumference | 14 in | 16½ in | 18½ in | 20¾ in | 23½ in |
| Finished height | 5 in | 6 in | 6¾ in | 7½ in | 9 in |
| Yarn amount | 99 yd | 137 yd | 170 yd | 219 yd | 279 yd |

Designed to be worn with no ease.

## materials:

* 1 (1, 2, 2, 2) x 3½ oz hanks of Malabrigo Twist (100% wool), Terron
* K/10½ hook

## yarn review:

This bulky-weight yarn lives up to its name, with great twist, making it hard-wearing with beautiful stitch definition.

## yarn alternative:

Wendy Mode Chunky

## gauge:

Work 13.5 sts and 11 rows in half double crochet in the back bar to measure 4 in square using K/10½ hook, or size needed to achieve gauge.

## special stitches:

**Half Double Crochet in the Back Bar (hdcb)**
YO the hook, insert the hook into the bar behind the back loop, YO and pull through the stitch (three loops on the hook), YO and pull through all the loops on the hook.

**Half Double Crochet in the Front Bar (hdcf)**
YO the hook, insert the hook into the bar in front of the front loop, YO and pull through the stitch (three loops on the hook), YO and pull through all loops on the hook.

## pattern notes:

The hat is worked from the top down in rounds. Do not count the t-ch at the beginning of the round as a stitch. Most of the hat is worked with the WS facing; do not turn the rounds unless specified.

## instructions:

**Rnd 1 (WS):** Working into magic loop (see Techniques, page 17), ch 2, 8hdc. Join.

**Rnd 2:** Ch2, *2hdcb in next st; rep from * around. Join. 16 sts.

**Rnd 3:** Ch2, *1hdcb, 2hdcb in next st; rep from * around. Join. 24 sts.

**Rnd 4:** Ch2, *2hdcb, 2hdcb in next st; rep from * around. Join. 32 sts.

**Rnd 5:** Ch2, *3hdcb, 2hdcb in next st; rep from * around. Join. 40 sts.

**Rnd 6:** Ch2, *4hdcb, 2hdcb in next st; rep from * around. Join. 48 sts.

### For sizes Baby, Toddler, Child and Adult ONLY

**Rnd 7:** Ch2, *5hdcb, 2hdcb in next st; rep from * around. Join. 56 sts.

### For sizes Toddler, Child and Adult ONLY

**Rnd 8:** Ch2, *6hdcb, 2hdcb in next st; rep from * around. Join. 64 sts.

### For sizes Child and Adult ONLY

**Rnd 9**: Ch2, *7hdcb, 2hdcb in next st; rep from * around. Join. 72 sts.

### For size Adult ONLY

**Rnd 10**: Ch2, *8hdcb, 2hdcb in next st; rep from * around. Join. 80 sts.

### For ALL sizes

**Rnd 1:** Ch2, 48 (56, 64, 72, 80) hdcb. Join. 48 (56, 64, 72, 80) sts.

Work Round 1 a total of 2 (4, 5, 0, 3) times.

### Pattern:

**Rnd 1:** Turn. Ch2, 48 (56, 64, 72, 80) hdcf. Join. Do not turn.

**Rnd 2:** Ch2, 48 (56, 64, 72, 80) hdcb. Join. Do not turn.

**Rnd 3:** Ch2, 48 (56, 64, 72, 80) hdcb. Join. Turn.

Work Rounds 1–3 a total of 2 (2, 2, 4, 4) times.

### Finishing

Block and weave in ends.

For a bolder "stripe" of stitches, turn your work
earlier to create a larger band of knit-look ridges.

# knitterly cowl

This cowl is very chunky, warm, and guaranteed to keep its recipient snuggly in the coldest of weathers.

## skill level **beginner**

| Size | One size |
|---|---|
| Finished height | 12½ in |
| Finished circumference | 27½ in |
| Yarn amount | 372 yd |

## materials:

* 3 x 3½ oz hanks Malabrigo Twist (100% wool), Terron
* K/10½ hook

## yarn review:

This is a beautiful bulky-weight yarn with a soft touch and crystal clear stitch definition.

## yarn alternatives:

Wendy Mode Chunky

## gauge:

Work 13.5 sts and 11 rows in half double crochet in the back bar to measure 4 in square using K/10½ hook, or size needed to achieve gauge.

## special stitches:

**Half Double Crochet in the Back Bar (hdcb)**
YO the hook, insert the hook into the bar behind the back loop, YO and pull through the stitch (three loops on the hook), YO and pull through all the loops on the hook.

**Half Double Crochet in the Front Bar (hdcf)**
YO the hook, insert the hook into the bar in front of the front loop, YO and pull through the stitch (three loops on the hook), YO and pull through all the loops on the hook.

## pattern notes:

Count the t-ch at the beginning of the round as a stitch.

There is no RS or WS to the pattern, with the stitch pattern being reversible.

## instructions:

Chain 95. Join for working in the round, being careful not to twist.

**Rnd 1 (RS):** Ch2, 95hdc. Join. Do not turn.

**Rnd 2:** Ch2, 95hdcb. Join. Do not turn.

**Rnd 3:** Ch2, 95hdcb. Join. Turn.

**Rnd 4:** Ch2, 95hdcf. Join. Do not turn.

**Rnd 5:** Ch2, 95hdcb. Join. Do not turn.

**Rnd 6:** Ch2, 95hdcb. Join. Turn.

Work Rounds 4–6 until the piece measures 12½ in from the beginning chain.

**Finishing**

Weave in the ends and block.

This pattern is easily adaptable. Chain a length you want the cowl. Join in the round and work in pattern until your cowl is wide enough.

# granite mitts

The reverse side of the common granite stitch is perfect for more unisex gifts. Combined with a silk blend yarn, these mitts are perfect for the refined men in your life.

## skill level **beginner**

| Size | Small | Medium | Large | Extra large |
|---|---|---|---|---|
| Finished circumference (a) | 6 in | 7 in | 7¼ in | 8 in |
| Finished length (b) | 6 in | 7 in | 7¾ in | 9 in |
| Yarn amount | 142 yd | 175 yd | 219 yd | 274 yd |

Designed to be worn with ¾ in negative ease.

## materials:

* 1 x 3½ oz hank Cadcade Venezia Sport, (70% merino wool, 30% mulberry silk), Ginger (160)
* F/5 hook
* Stitch marker

## yarn review:

A light and drapey sport-weight, this yarn has just a hint of sheen.

## yarn alternative:

MillaMia Naturally Soft Merino

## gauge:

Work 13 sts and 26 rows in granite stitch to measure 4 in square using F/5hook, or size needed to achieve gauge.

## special stitch:

**Granite Stitch (for swatch)**

Chain an even number of stitches.

**Row 1:** Starting with second ch from hook, 1 sc *ch 1, skip 1ch, 1 sc in next ch; rep from * to last ch, 2 sc. Turn.

**Row 2:** Ch 1, 1 sc, ch 1, skip next sc, *1 sc in next ch-space, ch 1, skip next sc; rep from * to last 2 sts, 1 sc in ch-space, 1 sc in sc. Turn. Work Row 2 until the piece measures at least 4in from the beginning chain.

## pattern note:

This pattern is worked in the round in the amigurumi style, with no seams or turning chains at the start of the rounds.

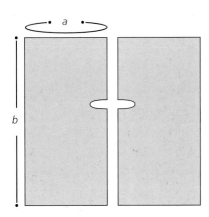

## instructions:

Chain 40 (44, 48, 52). Join for working in the round, being careful not to twist.

**Rnd 1:** Ch 1 (does not count as a st), 1 sc in same st, ch 1, skip next ch, *1 sc in next ch, ch 1, skip next ch; rep from * around, pm. Do not join. Do not turn. 20 (22, 24, 26) sc sts.

**Rnd 2:** *Skip next sc, ch 1, 1 sc in next ch-space; rep from * around.

Work Round 2 until the piece measures 3 (3½, 4, 4½) in, moving the stitch marker up with each round to mark the start of the round.

### Thumb Opening

**Rnd 1:** Ch 8 (8, 10, 10), skip next 4 (4, 5, 5) sc and 3 (3, 4, 4) ch, 1 sc in next ch-space, * skip next sc, ch 1, 1 sc in next ch-space; rep from * around. 16 (18, 19, 21) sc sts.

**Rnd 2:** [1 sc in ch, ch 1, skip next ch] 4 (4, 5, 5) times, * skip next sc, ch 1, 1 sc in next ch-space; rep from * around. 20 (22, 24, 26) sc sts.

**Rnd 3:** *Skip next sc, ch 1, 1 sc in next ch-space; rep from * around.

Work Round 3 until the piece measures 6 (7, 7¾, 9) in from the top, moving the stitch marker up with each round to mark the start of the round.

### Finishing

To finish, slip stitch into the next sc. Break yarn. Turn the mitts inside out and weave in the ends.

The stitch is shown with the wrong side facing. Simply make your tube as you normally would and turn the piece inside out at the end.

# leather and linen tablet case

There is just something about the combination of leather and yarn. This most basic of Tunisian stitches works beautifully with the leather, making a perfect gift.

## skill level **beginner**

| Size | Small | Large |
| --- | --- | --- |
| Finished height | 7¾ in | 9½ in |
| Finished width | 5¼ in | 7 in |
| Yarn amount | 77 yd | 131 yd |

## materials:

* 1x 3½ oz hank of Rowan Creative Linen (50% linen, 50% cotton), Natural
* H/8 Tunisian hook
* Leather punch
* 2 x 1¼ in wide leather buckle or belt

## yarn review:

This sport-weight linen cotton blend is hard-wearing and washable. It comes in a range of muted colors.

## yarn alternative:

King Cole Craft Cotton

## gauge:

Work 18 sts and 16 rows in Tunisian simple stitch to measure 4 in square using H/8 hook, or size needed to achieve gauge.

## special stitches:

See Techniques, page 18 for Tunisian simple stitch (tss) and standard return pass (srp).

*Recyle an old leather belt for the strap.*

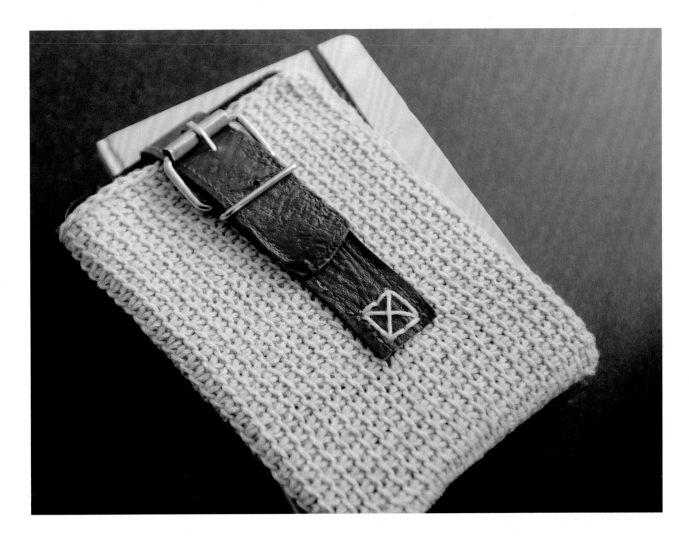

## instructions:

Chain 49 (65).

**Row 1:** Starting in second ch from hook, 48 (64) tss, srp. 48 (64) sts.

**Row 2:** 48 (64) tss, srp.

Work Row 2 until the piece measures 7¾ (9½) in.

With the yarn still attached, fold the work in half, WS together. Working through both layers of fabric, sl st the seam closed by working through the larger gaps left in between each tss. Break yarn.

Reattach the yarn at the side seam. Sl st the side seam closed. For the neatest finish, insert the hook into both sets of "chain" loops running along the edges of the rows. Break yarn.

### Straps

Using a leather punch on the smallest setting, punch holes around the outside of the bottom of the straps as shown.

Sew the strap into place, using the photograph as a guide—sewing one onto each side of the case.

# *everyone (needs) socks*

Don't just make socks for him. This pattern is sized so
you can make socks for, well, everyone!

## skill level **intermediate**

### Children

| Size | 6–12 months | 1–3 years | 3–5 years | 5–7 years | 7–13 years |
|---|---|---|---|---|---|
| Finished ankle size (a) | 4 in | 5½ in | 5½ in | 6½ in | 7 in |
| Finished foot length (b) | 4 in | 5 in | 6 in | 6¼ in | 7 in |
| Yarn amount | 112 yd | 241 yd | 241 yd | 306 yd | 372 yd |

| | Women | | | Men | | | |
|---|---|---|---|---|---|---|---|
| Size | Small | Medium | Large | 9 | 10 | 11 | 12 |
| Finished ankle size (a) | 7 in | 7¾ in | 9 in | 7 in | 7¾ in | 9 in | 10½ in |
| Finished foot length (b) | 9 in | 10 in | 11 in | 9½ in | 10½ in | 11in | 11½ in |
| Yarn amount | 449 yd | 547 yd | 635 yd | 471 yd | 569 yd | 657 yd | 710 yd |

Socks are designed to fit with 0-½ in negative ease.

**materials:**

* 1 (1, 1, 1, 1), 2 (2, 2, 2, 2, 2, 2) hanks
  of Artesano Definition Sock Yarn (75%
  wool, 25% nylon), Tornado
* D/3 hook
* 2 stitch markers

**yarn review:**

The nylon in this sock-weight yarn makes it
perfect for creating socks you can wear every
day.

**yarn alternative:**

Regia 6-ply Sock Yarn

**gauge:**

Work 20 sts and 20 rows in extended single
crochet to measure 4 in square using D/3
hook, or size needed to achieve gauge.

*Nothing says "I love you" more than taking the time to make something as everyday as a pair of socks.*

## special stitch:

**Extended Single Crochet (exsc)**

Insert the hook into the stitch, yarn over, pull through, yarn over, pull through the first loop on the hook, yarn over, pull through both loops on the hook.

## pattern notes:

Do not count the t-ch as a stitch. Directions for the adult sizes are shown in bold.

## instructions (make 2):

### Toe

Chain 5 (5, 7, 7, 9), **9 (11, 13, 11, 13, 13,13)**.

**Rnd 1:** Ch 1, 2 sc in second chain from hook, 2 (2, 4, 4, 6), **6 (8, 10, 8, 10, 10, 10)** sc, (2 sc, pm, 2 sc) into last ch, turning work as you go to work across other side of beg ch, 2 (2, 4, 4, 6), **6 (8, 10, 8, 10, 10, 10)** sc, 2 sc in last ch, pm. Join. 12 (12, 16, 16, 20), **20 (24, 28, 24, 28, 28, 28)** sts.

**Rnd 2:** Ch 1, 2 sc in first st, sc to 1 st before marker, 2 sc in sc, sm, 2 sc in sc, sc to 1 st before end of round, 2 sc in sc. Join. 16 (16, 20, 20, 24), **24 (28, 32, 28, 32, 32, 32)** sts. Work round 2 a total of 2 (4, 3, 4, 4), **4 (4, 4, 3, 3, 4, 6)** times. 20 (28, 28, 32, 36), **36 (40, 44, 36, 40, 44, 52)** sts.

### Foot

**Rnd 1:** Ch2, 20 (28, 28, 32, 36), **36 (40, 44, 36, 40, 44, 52)**exsc. Join. Work Round 1 until the piece measures 7 (10, 12, 13.5, 15), **20 (22.5, 25, 21, 23.5, 25, 26)** cm from the toe.

### Leg

**Rnd 1:** Ch2, 10 (14, 14, 16, 18), **18 (20, 22, 18, 20, 22, 26)** exsc, 10 (14, 14, 16, 18), **18 (20, 22, 18, 20, 22, 26)** fsc, skip 10 (14, 14, 16, 18), **18 (20, 22, 18, 20, 22, 26)** exsc. Join.

**Rnd 2:** Ch2, exsc in each fsc and exsc across. 20 (28, 28, 32, 36), **36 (40, 44, 36, 40, 44, 52)** sts. Work Round 2 until the leg measures 3 (3½,4,4½,5), **5½ (5½, 5½, 5½, 6, 6, 6)** in.

### Ribbing

**For Children's sizes ONLY**

Chain 3.

**Row 1:** Starting in second ch from hook, 3 sc, sl st into next 2 sts of leg. Turn. 3 sts.

**Row 2:** 3 sc in BLO. Turn.

**Row 3:** Ch 1, 3 sc in BLO, sl st into next 2 sts of leg. Turn.

Continue working Rows 2–3 around the leg until all the stitches are used. Slip stitch into the unworked side of the ribbing beginning chain to close. Break yarn.

**For Adult sizes ONLY**

Chain 6.

**Row 1:** Starting in second ch from hook, 6 sc, sl st into next 2 sts of leg. Turn. 6 sts.

**Row 2:** 6 dc in BLO. Turn.

**Row 3:** Ch 1, 6 sc in BLO, sl st into next 2 sts of leg. Turn.

Continue working Rows 2–3 around the leg until all the stitches are used. Slip stitch into the unworked side of the beginning chain to close. Break yarn.

## Afterthought Heel

Rejoin yarn at the first missed stitch of the gusset at the heel.

**Rnd 1:** Ch2 (does not count as a st), 10 (14, 14, 16, 18), **18 (20, 22, 18, 20, 22, 26)** sc, pm, 10 (14, 14, 16, 18), **18 (20, 22, 18, 20, 22, 26)** sc, pm. Join. 20 (28, 28, 32, 36), **36 (40, 44, 36, 40, 44, 52)** sts.

**Rnd 2:** Ch 1, 1 sc2tog, dc to 2 sts before marker, 1 sc2tog, sm, sc2tog, sc to 2 sts before end of round, sc2tog. Join. 16 (24, 24, 28, 32), **32 (36, 40, 32, 36, 40, 48)** sts.

**Rnd 3:** Work even in pattern.

Work Rounds 2 and 3 a total of 2 (4, 3, 4, 4), **4 (4, 4, 3, 3, 4, 6)** times. 12 (12, 16, 16, 20), **20 (24, 28, 24, 28, 28, 28)** sts.

## Finishing

Turn the sock inside out. Fold the heel in half with stitch markers at the corner, rm, sew or sl st the heel seam closed. Weave in the ends.

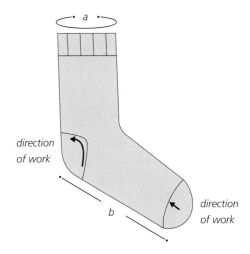

*direction of work*

*direction of work*

a

b

# shawl collar cardigan

This classic raglan shape with a nice thick shawl collar is the perfect gift for men in your life.

## skill level **intermediate**

| Finished chest circumference (a) | 38 in | 40 in | 42 in | 44 in | 46 in | 48 in | 50 in |
|---|---|---|---|---|---|---|---|
| Finished length (b) | 29 in | 30 in | 31 in | 31¾ in | 32½ in | 33½ in | 34½ in |
| Yarn amount | 837 yd | 903 yd | 985 yd | 1046 yd | 1111 yd | 1166 yd | 1248 yd |

Designed to be worn with 2 in positive ease.

## materials:

* 8 (9, 9, 10, 11, 11, 12) x 1¾ oz balls of Rico Essentials Merino (100% wool), Grey
* J/10 Tunisian hook
* 6 stitch markers
* 3 coat-style toggles

## yarn review:

This sport-weight superwash wool is luxuriously soft and hard-wearing.

## yarn alternative:

Artesano Superwash

## gauge:

Work 16 sts and 18 rows in Tunisian knit stitch to measure 4 in square using J/10 hook, or size needed to achieve gauge.

## special stitches:

See Techniques, page 18 for Tunisian simple stitch (tss), standard return pass (srp) and Tunisian knit stitch (tks).

**Tunisian Knit Stitch 2 Together (tks2tog)**
Insert the hook from left to right in each of the next two stitches, YO and pull through all the stitches.

## pattern note:

This cardigan is worked from the bottom up, with the shawl collar picked up at the end.

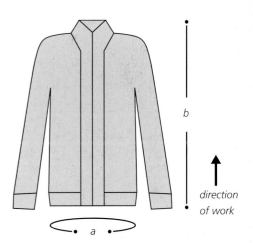

b

*direction of work*

a

*Tunisian knit stitch is one of the basic Tunisian stitches, creating a very warm, thick fabric.*

instructions:

### Sleeves (Make 2)

#### Cuff

Chain 31 (33, 35, 36, 38, 39, 41).

**Row 1:** Starting in second ch from hook, 30 (32, 34, 35, 37, 38, 40) tss, srp.

**Row 2:** 30 (32, 34, 35, 37, 38, 40) tss, srp.

Work Row 2 until the cuff measures 2 in.

#### Sleeve

**Row 1:** 1tks, 2tks in next, tks to 2sts from end, 2tks in next, 1tks, srp. 32 (34, 36, 37, 39, 40, 42) sts.

**Rows 2–5:** Tks across, srp.

Work Rows 1–5 a total of 10 (10, 11, 11, 12, 12, 13) times. 50 (52, 56, 57, 61, 62, 66) sts. Work even until the sleeve measures 18

(18½, 19, 19¾, 20, 20, 20½) in from the cuff. Seam the sleeve up the sides. Place the stitch marker 5 (6, 7, 8, 9, 20, 11) stitches away from the seam on both sides. 11 (13, 15, 17, 19, 21, 23) sts between markers (seam counts as 1 stitch).

### Body

#### Bottom Edging

Chain 135 (143, 151, 159, 167, 175, 183).

**Row 1:** Starting in second ch from hook, 134 (142, 150, 158, 166, 174, 182) tss, srp.

**Row 2:** 134 (142, 150, 158, 166, 174, 182) tss, srp.

Work Row 2 until the edging measures 2 in.

#### Body

**Row 1:** 134 (142, 150, 158, 166, 174, 182) tks, srp.

Work Row 1 until the piece measures 20½ (20¾, 21¾, 22, 22½, 22¾) in.

#### Join Sleeves

**Row 1:** 24 (25, 26, 27, 28, 29, 30) tks, pick up sleeve and 39 (39, 41, 40, 42, 41, 43) tks of sleeve, leaving marked armhole sts, skip 11 (13, 15, 17, 19, 21, 23) sts of body, work 64 (66, 68, 70, 72, 74, 76) tks across the back, pick up second sleeve, 39 (39, 41, 40, 42, 41, 43) tks of sleeve, leaving marked armhole sts, skip 11 (13, 15, 17, 19, 21, 23) sts of body, 24 (25, 26, 27, 28, 29, 30) tks, rp. 190 (194, 202, 204, 212, 214, 222) sts. Work even for 8 rows.

#### Decreases:

**Set-up row:** 24 (25, 26, 27, 28, 29, 30) tks,

pm in next, 37 (37, 39, 38, 40, 39, 41) tks, pm in next, 64 (66, 68, 70, 72, 74, 76) tks across the back, pm in next, 37 (37, 39, 38, 40, 39, 41) tks of sleeve, pm in next, 24 (25, 26, 27, 28, 29, 30) tks, srp. 190 (194, 202, 204, 212, 214, 222) sts.

**Row 1:** [Tks to 2 sts before pm, 1tks2tog, 1tks, 1tks2tog] four times, tks to end, srp. 182 (186, 194, 196, 204, 206, 214) sts.

**Row 2:** Tks across, srp.

Work Rows 1–2 a total of 18 (18, 19, 19, 20, 19, 20) times, 38 (42, 44, 46, 48, 56, 58) sts.

**Row 3:** Tks all the way across, srp, working

all sts and removing markers.

**Row 4:** Tks across, srp. Break yarn.

## Collar

Rejoin the yarn at the bottom front of the cardigan. Pick up a loop from each row end up the front, from each stitch around the neck and from each row end down the other side of the front, rp. 236 (242, 252, 256, 262, 268, 276) sts.

**Rows 1–8:** Tss across, srp. Break yarn and weave in the ends.

## Finishing

Sew up the opening at the underarms. For toggle loops, ch 30. Using the photograph for placement, sew toggles onto the front of the cardigan.

# Chapter 4

# For little ones

*******

Granny pixie hat
Pompom slippers
Kite bunting
First day of school socks
Breton top
Granny chevron blanket
Lacy yoke cardigan

# granny pixie hat

Using a traditional granny stripe pattern and a muted palette gives this baby hat a lovely vintage feel.

## skill level **beginner**

| Size | Newborn | Baby | Toddler | Child |
| --- | --- | --- | --- | --- |
| Finished hat height | 10 in | 12½ in | 14 in | 15 in |
| Finished hat depth | 12½ in | 16 in | 17 in | 18½ in |
| Yarn amount | 109 yd | 131 yd | 164 yd | 219 yd |

## materials:

* Color A: 1 x 7/8 oz ball from Mini Cakes Yarn Pack of Libby Summers Fine Aran (50% wool, 50% alpaca), Larama
* Color B: 1 x 7/8 oz ball from Mini Cakes Yarn Pack of Libby Summers Fine Aran (50% wool, 50% alpaca), Pante
* Color C: 1 x 7/8 oz ball from Mini Cakes Yarn Pack of Libby Summers Fine Aran (50% wool, 50% alpaca), Verde
* Color D: 1 x 7/8 oz ball from Mini Cakes Yarn Pack of Libby Summers Fine Aran (50% wool, 50% alpaca), Lima
* Color E: 1 x 7/8 oz ball from Mini Cakes Yarn Pack of Libby Summers Fine Aran (50% wool, 50% alpaca), Kulli
* Color F: 1 x 7/8 oz ball from Mini Cakes Yarn Pack of Libby Summers Fine Aran (50% wool, 50% alpaca), Azule
* G/6 hook

## yarn review:

This luscious wool and alpaca blend yarn is soft and perfect for wearing next to the skin.

## yarn alternative:

King Cole Merino Blend Aran

## gauge:

Work 5 clusters and 9 rows in pattern to measure 4 in square using G/6 hook, or size needed to achieve gauge.

## special stitch:

**Granny Stripe**

For swatching, chain 21 and follow instructions for Rows 1–3. Then work Rows 2 and 3 a total of four times.

## pattern notes:

Count the turning chain as a stitch. Change colors at the start of each row, working in sequence with Colors A–F as you work each row.

*Even in larger sizes, this hat works up quickly and easily for last-minute gift giving.*

## instructions:

With Color A, ch 45 (54, 60, 63).

**Row 1:** Starting in sixth ch from hook (counts as 1 dc and ch 1), [3 dc in next ch, ch 1, skip ch 2] 13 (16, 18, 19) times, 1 dc. Turn. Break yarn. 13 (16, 18, 19) 3 dc clusters.

**Row 2:** Attach new color, ch 3, 2 dc in ch-space, [ch 1, skip 3 dc, 3 dc in ch-space] 12 (15, 17, 18) times, 2 dc in ch-space, 1 dc in top of t-ch. Turn. Break yarn. 14 (17, 19, 20) 3 dc clusters.

**Row 3:** Attach new color, ch 5, skip 3 dc, [3 dc in ch-space, ch 1, skip 3 dc] 13 (16, 18, 19) times, 1 dc. Turn. Break yarn. 13 (16, 18, 19) 3 dc clusters.

Work Rows 2–3 a total of 7 (9, 9, 10) times. For sizes toddler and child, work Row 2 once more.

Fold the beginning chain in half widthwise and sew or sl st the seam closed.

### Bottom Edging

**Row 1:** With Color A, chain 10 (11, 12, 13), attach to front bottom edge of hat. Sc around bottom of hat; 1 sc into each t-ch and/or dc around, 11 (12, 13, 14) ch. Turn. 28 (36, 38, 42) sts.

**Row 2:** Starting in second ch from hook, 48 (58, 62, 68) sc across ch and sc. Break yarn.

### Pompoms (Make 2)

Cut a 12 in piece of contrast yarn and set it aside.

Using the yarn still attached to the ball, secure the cut end of yarn between two of your fingers, take your contrast yarn and wrap it approximately 60 times around your non-dominant hand.

Carefully remove the yarn from your fingers. Pick up the set-aside yarn and wrap it widthwise around the loops of yarn. Tie it off tightly.

Cut the loops, being careful not to cut the securing tie. Fluff up the yarn and trim into a pompom shape.

Sew securely to each end of the ties on the hat.

**Note:** Pompoms can come undone and present a choking hazard with loose strands of yarn. Under-threes should not be left unattended with pompoms. If in doubt, leave them off.

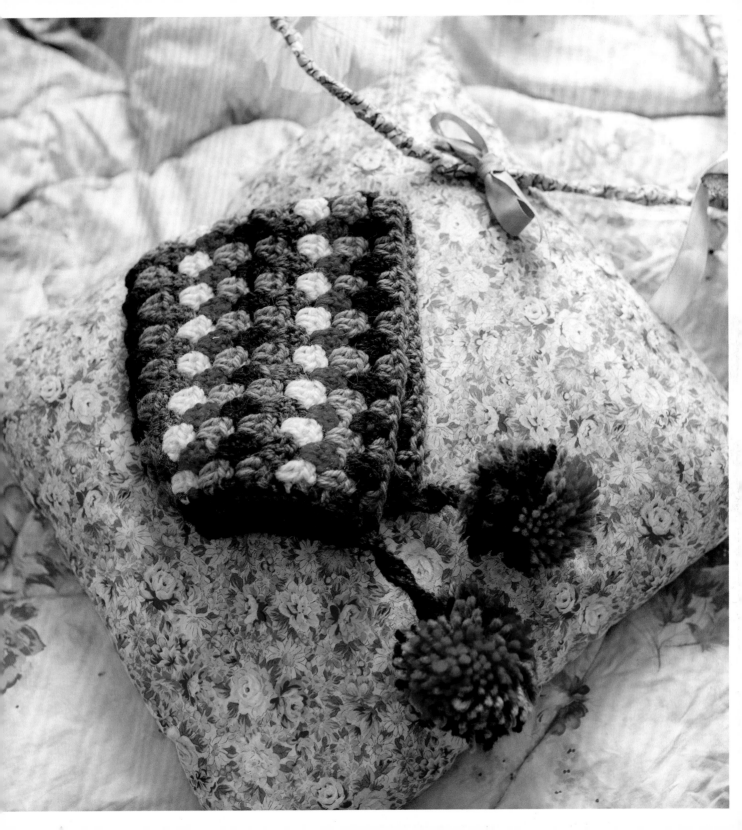

# pompom slippers

Inspired by a pair of sewn booties we were given when our son Ellis was a baby, these have become the go-to gift for new babies in our lives.

## skill level **advanced beginner**

| Size | 6–12 months | 1–3 years | 3–5 years | 5–7 years | 7–13 years |
|---|---|---|---|---|---|
| Finished foot circumference | 4½ in | 5½ in | 6 in | 6½ in | 7 in |
| Finished length | 4 in | 5 in | 6 in | 6½ in | 7 in |
| Yarn amount: main colour | 71 yd | 115 yd | 142 yd | 176 yd | 208 yd |
| Yarn amount: contrast colour | 33 yd | 33 yd | 33 yd | 33 yd | 33 yd |

Designed to be worn with no ease.

**materials:**

* Main Color (MC): 1 x 1¾ oz ball of Brown Sheep Nature Spun Sport (100% wool), Charcoal
* Contrast Color (CC): 1 x 1¾ oz ball of Brown Sheep Nature Spun Sport (100% wool), Flamingo (also pictured in Turquoise Wonder)
* F/5 hook
* Sew-on snaps
* Stitch marker
* Safety pins

**yarn review:**
This high-twist 100% wool yarn is hardwearing—perfect for busy feet. It also comes in an astounding array of colors, so you will be able to choose your palette.

**yarn alternative:**
Rowan Felted Tweed 4 ply

**gauge:**
Work 22 sts and 24 rows in double crochet to measure 4 in square using F/5 hook, or size needed to achieve gauge.

**pattern note:**
Do not count turning chains as a stitch.

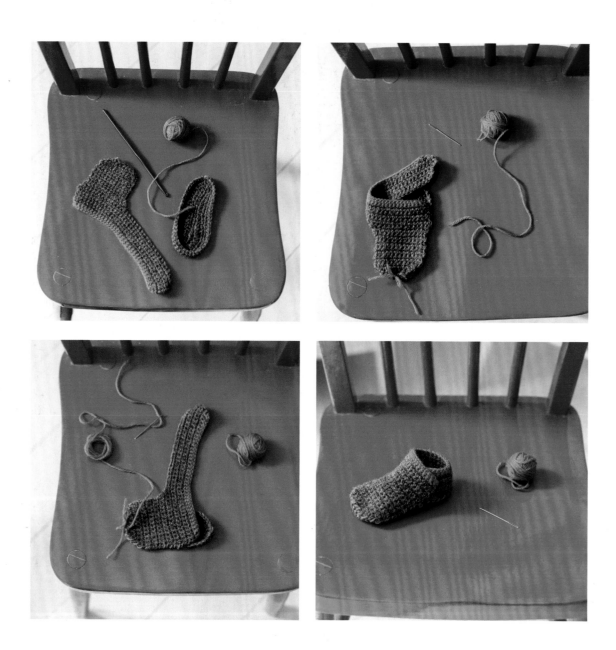

Add a bit of liquid rubber to the soles to make the slippers
non-skid for walkers and crawlers.

## instructions:

### Soles (Make 2)

With MC, ch 17 (18, 21, 22, 22).

**Rnd 1:** Starting in second ch from hook, 2 sc in next ch, 4 (4, 5, 5, 5) sc, 6 (7, 8, 8, 8) hdc, 4 (4, 5, 6, 6) dc, 4 dc in last ch; turning work to work down unworked side of beg ch, 4 (4, 5, 6, 6) dc, 6 (7, 8, 8, 8) hdc, 4 (4, 5, 5, 5) sc, 2 sc in last ch (this already has 2 sc worked into it). Join. 36 (38, 44, 46, 46) sts.

**Rnd 2:** Ch 1, [2 sc in next sc] twice, 14 (15, 18, 19, 19) sc, [2 sc in next dc] four times, 14 (15, 18, 19, 19) sc, [2 sc in next sc] twice. Join. 44 (46, 52, 54, 54) sts.

**Rnd 3:** Ch 1, 1 sc, pm, 2 sc in next sc, 18 (19, 22, 23, 23) sc, 2 sc in next st, pm, 2 sc, 2 sc in next st, 18 (19, 22, 23, 23) sc, 2 sc in next st, pm, 1 sc. Join. 48 (50, 56, 58, 58) sts.

### For sizes 1–3 years, 3–5 years, 5–7 years and 7–13 years ONLY

**Rnd 4:** 1 sc, 2 sc in next, work to 1 st from marker, 2 sc in next sc, 2 sc, 2 sc in next sc, work to 2 sts from end of round, 2 sc in next sc, 1 sc. Join.

Work Round 4 a total of – (1, 2, 4, 5) times. Break yarn. – (54, 64, 74, 78) sts.

### Left Upper

With CC, ch 37 (42, 45, 48, 51).

**Row 1 (RS):** Starting in second ch from hook, 36 (41, 44, 47, 50) sc. Turn. Switch to MC; work 5 (7, 11, 15, 17) rows as follows: Ch 1, 36 (41, 44, 47, 50) sc. Turn. Work 24 (29, 38, 47, 51) rows as follows: ch 1, 15 (18, 20, 21, 23) sc. Turn. 15 (18, 20, 21, 23) sts.

**Next row:** Ch 1, 1 sc2tog, 11 (14, 16, 17, 19) sc, 1 sc2tog. Turn. 13 (16, 18, 19, 21) sts.

**Next row:** Ch 1, 1 sc2tog, 9 (12, 14, 15, 17) sc, 1 sc2tog. Turn. Break yarn. 11 (14, 16, 17, 19) sts.

### Right Upper

With CC, ch 37 (42, 45, 48, 51).

**Row 1 (RS):** Starting in second ch from hook, 36 (41, 44, 47, 50) sc. Turn. Switch to MC; work 5 (7, 11, 15, 17) rows as follows: Ch 1, 36 (41, 44, 47, 50) sc. Turn. Break yarn.

**Next row:** Skip 21 (23, 24, 26, 27) sc, rejoin MC, ch 1, 15 (18, 20, 21, 23) sc. Turn. 15 (18, 20, 21, 23) sts.

Work 23 (28, 37, 46, 50) rows as follows: Ch 1, 15 (18, 20, 21, 23) sc.

**Next row:** Ch 1, 1 sc2tog, 11 (14, 16, 17, 19) sc, 1 sc2tog. Turn. 13 (16, 18, 19, 21) sts.

**Next row:** Ch 1, 1 sc2tog, 9 (12, 14, 15, 17) sc, 1 sc2tog. Turn. Break yarn. 11 (14, 16, 17, 19) sts.

### Sewing Up

Line up the toe of the upper with the toe of the sole. Secure with a pin or a piece of string. Using CC, sew the two pieces together using a whipstitch. Sew around the bottom as shown, bringing the long end of the upper around inside the bootie.

Separate the snap and sew one side to the inside of the outer flap that wraps around the ankle and the other side onto the outside of the inner ankle flap. Make two small pompoms (see Techniques, page 21) and sew on using the photograph for placement.

# kite bunting

This pattern only needs small amounts of yarn in each color, so raid your stash to make a colorful and fun bunting.

## skill level **beginner**

| Size | One size |
|---|---|
| Finished length of motif | 4 in |
| Finished width of motif | 2¼ in |

**materials:**

* 1 x 1¾ oz ball Artesano Superwash (100% wool), Navy (6416)
* 1 x 1¾ oz ball Artesano Superwash (100% wool), Sand Yellow (7254)
* 1 x 1¾ oz ball Artesano Superwash (100% wool), Grey (SFN41)
* 1 x 1¾ oz ball Artesano Superwash (100% wool), Teal (5167)
* small amount of Artesano Superwash (100% wool), Cream (SFNIU)
* G/6 hook
* Tapestry needle

**yarn review:**

This is a fantastic superwash yarn that is a staple in my yarn stash.

**yarn alternatives:**

Cascade 220
Debbie Bliss Rialto DK

**gauge:**

1 motif measures 4 in x 2¼ in using G/6 hook, or size needed to achieve gauge.

**pattern note:**

Count the chains at the beginning of the round as a stitch.

*Hang high over a window to bring a bit of the outside in.*

## instructions:

**Kite (Make 5 to make a 39 in length of bunting)**

**Rnd 1:** Starting with magic loop (see Techniques, page 17), ch 3, 1 dc, [ch 2, 2 dc] three times, ch 1, 2 dc, ch 2, 2 dc, ch 1. Join with sl st into top of ch 3. 6 2 dc clusters.

**Rnd 2:** Sl st to first ch2-space, (ch 3, 1 dc, ch 2, 2 dc) into ch2-space, ch 1, [(2 dc, ch 2, 2 dc) into next ch2-space, ch 1] twice, 2 dc into ch1-space, ch 1, (2 dc, ch 2, 2 dc) into ch2-space, ch 1, 2 dc into ch1-space, ch 1. Join with sl st into the top of first dc. 10 2 dc clusters.

**Rnd 3:** Sl st to first ch2-space, (ch 3, 1 dc, ch 2, 2 dc) into ch2-space, [ch 1, 2 dc into ch1-space, ch 1, (2 dc, ch 2, 2 dc) into ch2-space] twice, [ch 1, 2 dc into ch1-space] twice, ch

1, (2 dc, ch 2, 2 dc) into ch2-space, [ch 1, 2 dc into ch1-space] twice, ch 1. Join with sl st into top of ch 3. 14 2 dc clusters.

**Rnd 4:** Sl st to first ch2-space, (ch 3, 1 dc, ch 2, 2 dc) into ch2-space, [(ch 1, 2 dc) into next ch1-space] twice, [ch 1, (2 dc, ch 2, 2 dc) into ch2-space] twice, [ch 1, 2 dc in next ch1-space] three times, ch 1, (2 dc, ch 2, 2 dc) into ch2-space, [ch 1, 2 dc into next ch1-space] three times, ch 1. Join with sl st into top of first dc. 18 2 dc clusters.

**Bows (Make 3 per kite in alternate colors)**

Ch 6.

**Row 1:** Starting in second stitch from hook,

5 sc. Turn. 5 sc.

**Rows 2–3:** Ch 1, 5 sc. Turn.

Break the yarn, leaving a 4 in tail. Weave the end into the middle of the last row and wrap it tightly around the middle of the piece to make a secure bow.

**Tail**

Thread three bows onto a 4in length of yarn, securing each one in place with a knot. Secure the yarn onto the bottom of the motif.

**Stringing**

With the yarn for string, ch 10, [1 sc into top ch2-space of motif, 10sc] five times. 10ch.

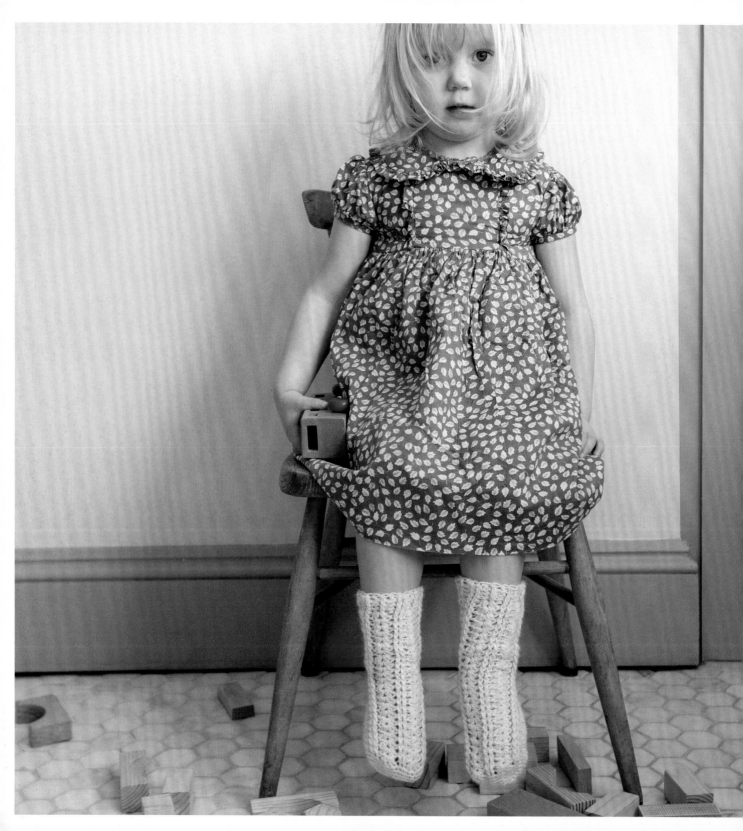

# first day of school socks

Send a bit of handmade love with them on their first big
day of school—from nursery to college.

## skill level **intermediate**

| Size | Baby | Child | Teen | Women's small | Women's large |
|------|------|-------|------|---------------|---------------|
| Finished ankle circumference (a) | 4¾ in | 6 in | 7 in | 8¼ in | 9½ in |
| Finished foot length (b) | 4 in | 6 in | 7 in | 10 in | 11 in |
| Yarn amount: | 197 yd | 241 yd | 317 yd | 438 yd | 591 yd |

Designed to be worn with no ease to ¾ in negative ease.

## materials:
* 1 (2, 2, 3, 3) x 1¾ oz balls of The Fibre
  Company Canopy (50% alpaca, 30%
  Merino, 20% Bamboo), Orchid
* F/5 hook
* 2 stitch markers
* Tapestry needle

## yarn review:
This has to be one of the most gorgeous sock
yarns I have ever laid hands on. The bamboo
adds sheen and strength to the luxurious
softness of the wool and alpaca.

## yarn alternative:
Artesano Definition Sock

## gauge:
Work 20 sts and 20 rows in single crochet to
measure 4 in square using F/5 hook, or size
needed to achieve gauge.

## special stitches:
### Short Row Single Crochet 2 Together (srsc2tog)
Insert the hook into the stitch at the end of
the row, yarn over and pull through, insert
hook into the first stitch of the longer row
below, yarn over and pull through. Yarn over,
pull through all three loops on the hook. Pull
tight to close off any gaps.

### Extended Single Crochet (exsc)
Insert the hook into the stitch, YO, pull
through, YO, pull through the first loop on
the hook, YO, pull through both loops on
the hook.

## pattern note:
Do not count the turning chain as a stitch.

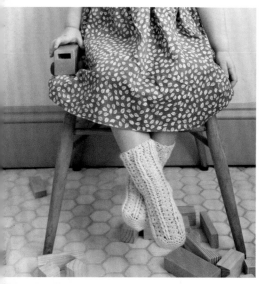

## instructions:

### Leg Ribbing

Leaving a 4 in tail for sewing up the gap, 20 (25, 30, 35, 40) fdc. Join for working in the round.

### Ribbing:

**Rnds 1–3 (3, 4, 4, 4):** Ch3 (does not count as a st), *1bpdc, 1fpdc, 1bpdc, 2fpdc; rep from * around. Join into top of ch 3.

### Pattern:

**Rnd 1:** Ch3, *skip 1 st, (2 dc, ch 1, 2 dc) in next, skip 1 st, 2fpdc; rep from * around. Join.

**Rnd 2:** Ch3, *skip 2 dc, (2 dc, ch 1, 2 dc) in ch-space, skip 2 dc, 2fpdc; rep from * around. Join.

Work Round 2 until the piece measures 4 (4¼, 5, 6, 7) in.

### Heel Flap

**Row 1 (RS):** Ch2 (does not count as a st), 2 sc, [skip ch-space, 6 sc] 1 (2, 2, 3, 3) times, 2 sc. Turn. 10 (16, 16, 22, 22) sts.

**Rows 2–6 (10, 10, 14, 14):** Ch 1, 10 (16, 16, 22, 22) sc. Turn.

### Heel Turn

**Row 1 (RS):** Ch 1, 7 (11, 11, 15, 15) sc. Turn.

**Row 2:** Ch 1, 4 (6, 6, 8, 8) sc. Turn.

**Row 3:** Ch 1, 3 (5, 5, 7, 7), 1srsc2tog. Turn. Rep Row 3 until all the stitches in the heel flap row are worked, ending on a RS row. 4 (6, 6, 8, 8) sts.

### Foot

**Set-up round (RS):** Ch2 (does not count as

a st), 4 (6, 6, 8, 8) exsc. Working up sides of heel flap, evenly place 4 (6, 9, 8, 11) exsc, 2fpdc, [skip 2 dc, (2 dc, ch 1, 2 dc) in ch-space, skip 2 dc, 2fpdc] 2 (2, 3, 3, 4) times. Working down sides of heel flap, evenly place 4 (6, 9, 8, 11) exsc. Join. Do not turn. 26 (32, 44, 44, 56) sts.

**Rnd 1:** Ch2, 8 (12, 15, 16, 19) exsc, fpdc, [skip 2 dc, (2 dc, ch 1, 2 dc) in ch-space, skip 2 dc, 2fpdc] 2 (2, 3, 3, 4) times, 4 (6, 9, 8, 11) exsc. Join.

Repeat round 1 until the sock measures 3¼ (5, 5¾, 8½, 9) in from the back of the heel.

### Toe

This section is worked in the amigurumi style with no joining or raising of the rounds.

**Set-up round:** Ch 1 (does not count as a st), 12 (16, 19, 20, 23) sc, [skip next ch-space, 6 sc] 1 (1, 2, 2, 3) times, 8 (10, 13, 12, 15) sc. Join. 26 (32, 44, 44, 56) sts.

**Rnd 1:** Ch 1, 13 (16, 22, 22, 28) sc, pm, 13

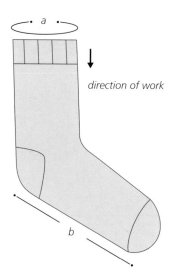

*a*

*direction of work*

*b*

(16, 22, 22, 28) sc, pm. Join.

**Rnd 2:** Ch 1, 1 sc2tog, work to 2 sts before marker, 1 sc2tog, sm, 1 sc2tog, work to 2 sts before end, 1 sc2tog. Join.

Repeat Round 2 until you have 14 (16, 16, 16, 16) sc remaining.

### Making Up

Fold the toe in half and seam the bottom and top together from the inside. Sew up the gap at the cuff. Weave in the ends.

*Short row heels can be tricky at first, but don't let them put you off—they have magical properties, turning a flap into a heel neatly and evenly.*

# breton top

This scrumptious little top is a simple and sweet make.

## skill level **intermediate**

| Size | 6 months | 18 months | 2 years | 4 years | 6 years | 8 years |
|---|---|---|---|---|---|---|
| Finished chest circumference (a) | 17¼ in | 19 in | 20¾ in | 23¼ in | 24¼ in | 26¼ in |
| Finished length (b) | 8¾ in | 10 in | 10½ in | 11 in | 11½ in | 12¼ in |
| Yarn amounts (MC) | 361 yd | 378 yd | 405 yd | 607 yd | 673 yd | 876 yd |

Designed to be worn with 0-½in positive ease.

## materials:

* Main Color (MC): 3 (3, 3, 4, 4, 5) x 1¾ oz balls of MillaMia (100% wool), Navy
* Contrast Color (CC): 1 x 1¾ oz balls of MillaMia (100% wool), White
* G/6 hook
* Tapestry needle
* 4 (4, 4, 5, 5, 6) buttons ½ in in diameter

## yarn review:

This sport-weight wool is washable and light, making it an excellent choice for children's clothes.

## yarn alternatives:

Cascade 220 Superwash Sport
Brown Sheep Nature Spun Sport

## gauge:

Work 16 sts and 11 rows in paired double crochet to measure 4 in square using G/6 hook, or size needed to achieve gauge.

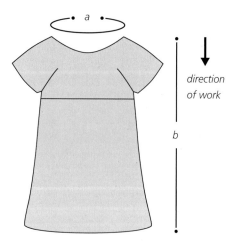

*a*

*direction of work*

*b*

## special stitches:

**Paired Double Crochet (pdc)**

**For Swatch:**

Chain an odd number of stitches.

**Row 1:** 1 sc in third ch from hook, 1 sc in same ch, *skip 1ch, 2 dc into next ch; repeat from * to last 2 sts, skip 1ch, 1 dc. Turn.

**Row 2:** Ch3 (counts as 1 dc), *2 dc in space between 2 dc; rep from * across 1 dc into top
of t-ch.

Work Row 2 until the piece measures at least 4 in from the beginning chain.

**Linked Double Crochet (ldc)**

Insert the hook into the middle loop of the stitch just worked, YO, pull the loop through, hook into the next stitch, YO, pull the loop through, YO, pull the loop through two loops on the hook, YO, pull through the last two loops.

**Linked Double Crochet after 3 Chain**

Insert the hook into the middle chain, YO, pull the loop through, hook into the next stitch, YO, pull the loop through, YO, pull the loop through two loops on the hook, YO, pull through the last two loops.

## pattern notes:

Count the t-ch as a stitch.

The bodice is designed to be quite fitted. For more ease, go up a size or work an extra repeat of bodice Rows 2 and 3.

## instructions:

**Bodice**

Chain 40 (42, 42, 44, 44, 44).

**Set-up row (WS):** Starting in fourth ch from hook (counts as 1 dc), 3ldc, [skip 1 dc, 2 dc in next st] twice, 1 dc, [skip 1 dc, 2 dc in next st] twice, 1 dc, [skip 1 dc, 2 dc in next st] 5 (6, 6, 7, 7, 7) times, 1 dc, [skip 1 dc, 2 dc in next st] twice, 1 dc, [skip 1 dc, 2 dc in next st] twice, 4ldc. Turn. 38 (40, 40, 42, 42, 42) sts.

**Row 1 (RS):** Ch3, 3ldc, skip dc, 2 dc in sp bet 2 dc, skip 2 dc, 4 dc in sp bet 2 dc, skip 1 dc, 1fpdc, [skip 1 dc, 4 dc in sp bet 2 dc, skip 1 dc] twice, 1fpdc, skip 1 dc, 4 dc in sp bet 2 dc, skip 1 dc, [skip 1 dc, 2 dc in sp bet 2 dc, skip 1 dc ] 3 (4, 4, 5, 5, 5) times, skip 1 dc, 4 dc in sp bet 2 dc, skip 1 dc, 1fpdc, [skip 1 dc, dc in sp bet 2 dc, skip 1 dc] twice, 1fpdc, skip 1 dc, 4 dc in sp bet 2 dc, skip 2 dc, 2 dc in sp bet 2 dc, 4ldc. Turn. 54 (56, 56, 58, 58, 58) sts.

**Row 2 and all WS rows:** Ch3, 3ldc, work pdc into each pdc and 1bpdc into each fpdc across, 4ldc.

**Row 3:** Ch3, 3ldc, *skip 1 dc, 2 dc in sp bet 2 dc, skip 1 dc; rep from * to 2 dc before bpdc, skip 1 dc, 4 dc in sp bet 2 dc, skip 1 dc, fpdc, [skip 1 dc, 4 dc in sp bet 2 dc, skip 1 dc, **skip 1 dc, 2 dc in sp bet 2 dc, skip 1 st; rep from ** to 2 dc before bpdc, skip 1 dc, 4 dc in sp bet 2 dc, skip 1 st, fpdc] three times, ^skip 1 dc, 2 dc in sp bet 2 dc, skip 1 dc; rep from ^ to ldc, 4ldc. Turn. 62 (64, 64, 66, 66, 66) sts. Work Rows 2 and 3 a total of 2 (3, 4, 4, 5, 5) times. 86 (96, 104, 106, 114, 114) sts.

Work even in pattern for 4 (1, 2, 4, 4, 6) rows.

**Joining work in the round:**

With RS facing, overlap the two sections of ldc, with the left side of the yoke to the front. Working through both layers of fabric, ch 3 (does not count as a stitch), 3 dc, *skip 1 dc, 2 dc in sp bet 2 dc, skip 1 dc; rep from * to fpdc, skip fpdc, 10 (10, 10, 14, 18, 20) fdc, skip fpdc, skip 16 (20, 20, 20, 24, 24)dc, *skip 1 dc, 2 dc in sp bet 2 dc, skip 1 dc; rep from * to fpdc, skip fpdc, 10 (10, 10, 14, 18, 20) fdc, mis fpdc, skip 16 (20, 20, 20, 24, 24) dc, skip next fpdc, *skip 1 dc, 2 dc in sp bet 2 dc, skip 1 dc; rep from * to beginning. Join.

Break the yarn and rejoin under the middle of the right armhole. 74 (76, 84, 94, 102, 106) sts.

**Body**

**Row 1:** Using MC, ch 3 (counts as 1 dc), 2 dc in each dc around. Join 148 (152, 168, 188, 204, 212) sts.

**Row 2:** Ch3, 1 dc in each stitch around. Join.

**Row 3:** Using CC, ch 1 (does not count as a st), 1 sc in each dc around. Join.

Work Rows 1–3 a total of 9 (9, 12, 15, 15, 18) times.

**Finishing**

Using the beginning chains from the yoke as buttonholes, evenly space your buttons on the edge of the opening and sew securely. Weave in the ends.

*Light and floaty, this is a perfect top to wear over jeans-or make the striped section longer for a dress.*

# granny chevron blanket

Strongly inspired by quilts, granny squares get a seriously modern update with this twist on granny square blankets.

## skill level **beginner**

| Size | Throw | Single bed | Double bed |
| --- | --- | --- | --- |
| Width | 35½ in | 70 in | 83 in |
| Length | 35½ in | 89 in | 89 in |
| Colour A | 482 yd | 2058 yd | 2286 yd |
| Colour B | 482 yd | 2168 yd | 2406 yd |

The photos show throw size.

## materials:
* Color A: 4 (17, 19) x 3½ oz balls of Texere Chunky Wool (100% wool), Slate
* Color B: 4 (18, 20) x 3½ oz balls of Texere Chunky Wool (100% wool), Mustard
* I/9 hook

## yarn review:
This bulky wool is 100% British and comes in a range of gorgeous colors.

## yarn alternatives:
Artesano British Wool Chunky
Wendy Mode Chunky

## gauge:
Work one granny square motif to measure 6 in square.

## pattern notes:
For each color change, drop the working color and pick up the new color. Leave the dropped color where it hangs. You will come back to it in the second half of the next round.
Count the ch 3 at the beginning of each round as 1 dc.

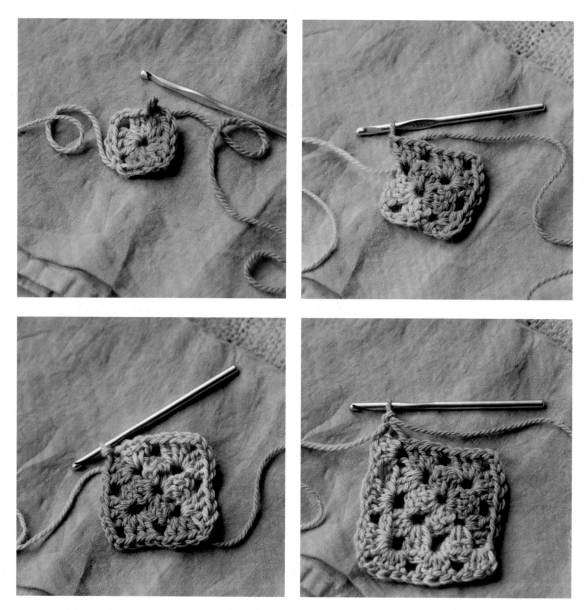

*For further layout inspiration, look to quilting resources for Half Square Triangles.*

## special technique:

### Switching Colors (switch to)

To give the neatest switch between colors: Leaving one loop of working yarn on the hook, pick up the next color, ch 2 only with the new color, YO, pull through both the old color and the new color loops on the hook.

## instructions:

### Granny Square

Chain 36 (180, 210).

With Color A, ch 3. Join in the round with a sl st.

**Rnd 1:** Working into center of ch 3 loop, ch 3 (counts as 1 dc), 2 dc, ch 2, 3 dc, ch 2, leaving 1 loop on hook, join Color B, ch 2 and YO, pull through both loops on hook (counts as 1 dc), 2 dc, ch 2, 3 dc, ch 2. Join with sl st into top of ch 3. Turn.

**Rnd 2:** Continuing with Color B, sl st to center of ch2-space, (ch 3, 2 dc) into ch-space, ch 1, (3 dc, ch 2, 3tr) into next ch-space, (3 dc, ch 2, switch to Color A, (ch 3 (counts as 1 dc) 2 dc) into next ch-space, ch 1, (3 dc, ch 2, 3 dc) into next ch-space, ch 1, (3 dc, ch 2) into ch-space you started the round with. Join into top of ch 3. Turn.

**Rnd 3:** Continuing with Color A, sl st to center of ch2-space, (ch 3, 2 dc) into ch-space, ch 1, 3 dc in next ch-space, ch 1, (3 dc, ch 2, 3 dc) in next ch-space, ch 1, 3 dc in next ch-space, ch 1, (3 dc, ch 1, switch to Color B, ch 1, 3 dc) in next ch-space, ch 1, 3 dc in next ch-space, ch 1, (3 dc, ch 2, 3 dc) in next ch-space, ch 1, 3 dc in next ch-space, ch 1, (3 dc, ch 2) into ch-space you started the round with. Join into top of ch 3. Turn.

**Rnd 4:** Continuing with Color B, sl st to center of ch2-space, (ch 3, 2 dc) into ch-space, [ch 1, 3 dc in next ch-space] twice, ch 1, (3 dc, ch 2, 3 dc) in next ch-space, [ch 1, 3 dc in next ch-space] twice, ch 1, (3 dc, ch 1, switch to Color A, ch 1, 3 dc) in next ch-space, [ch 1, 3 dc in next ch-space] twice, ch 1, (3 dc, ch 2, 3 dc) in next ch-space, [ch 1, 3 dc in next ch-space] twice, ch 1, (3 dc, ch 2) into ch-space you started the round with. Join into top of ch 3.

### Assembling

Using the illustrations as a guide, align the squares in pattern.

* The throw is laid out six squares wide by six squares tall.

* The single blanket is laid out 12 squares wide by 15 squares tall.

* The double blanket is laid out 14 squares wide by 15 squares tall.

Join the granny squares in vertical rows. Place two squares RS together. Starting in one corner, working through both sets of stitches, sc into each dc and ch-space across until you come to the next corner. Pick up another two squares, hold them RS together and continue working in the same way until all of the stitches are worked. Work in this manner until the entire first row is joined. Work the following rows by aligning one square to the opposite side of the already joined squares. Continue in this manner until all of the vertical rows are worked. Join the horizontal rows by aligning adjacent squares and sc into each dc and ch-space across.

single bed

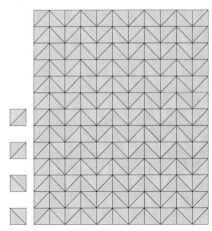

throw

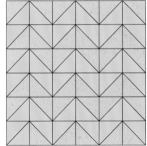

### Edging

**Rnd 1:** Join Color B to corner of blanket, ch 1, work 1 sc into each dc and ch-space around. Work (2 sc, ch 3, 2 sc) into each of four corners of joined blanket. Join into first sc with sl st.

**Rnd 2:** 1 sc in each sc around. Work (2 sc, ch 3, 2 sc) into each of four corners of joined blanket. Join into first sc with sl st.

# lacy yoke cardigan

Sweet lace at the collar creates impact on this pretty little pattern.

## skill level **intermediate**

| Size | Newborn | Baby | 1–2 years | 2 years | 4 years | 6 years | 8 years | 10 years |
|---|---|---|---|---|---|---|---|---|
| To fit chest (a) | 16½ in | 17¾ in | 19 in | 20¾ in | 22¾ in | 25¼ in | 26¾ in | 28¼ in |
| Length (b) | 8¼ in | 9 in | 10 in | 11 in | 11¾ in | 13 in | 15 in | 16½ in |
| Main colour | 192 yd | 224 yd | 263 yd | 317 yd | 383 yd | 454 yd | 564 yd | 651 yd |
| Contrast colour | 94 yd | 115 yd | 131 yd | 159 yd | 192 yd | 224 yd | 279 yd | 328 yd |

Cardigan is sized to be worn with 2in positive ease.

## materials:

* Color A: 2 (2, 3, 3, 4, 4, 5, 6) 1¾ oz balls of Artesano Superwash DK (100% wool), Sand Yellow
* Color B: 1 (1, 1, 2, 2, 2, 3, 3) 1¾ oz balls of Artesano Superwash DK (100% wool), Grey
* H/8 hook
* 8 (9, 10, 10, 11, 12, 15, 16) buttons ½ in in diameter
* 5 stitch markers

## gauge:

Work 8 sts and 4.5 rows in linked doubles to measure 4 in square using H/8 hook, or size needed to achieve gauge.

## special stitches:

**Linked Double Crochet (ldc)**

Insert the hook into the middle loop of the stitch just worked, YO, pull the loop through, hook into the next stitch, YO, pull the loop through, YO, pull the loop through two loops on the hook, YO, pull through the last two loops.

**Linked Double Crochet after 3 Chain**

Insert the hook into the middle chain, YO, pull the loop through, hook into the next stitch, YO, pull the loop through, YO, pull the loop through two loops on the hook, YO, pull through the last color two loops.

*For a more subtle design, make the cardigan all in one color.*

Count the t-ch at the beginning of each row as a stitch.

## instructions:

### Lace Collar and Yoke

With Color A, ch 55 (60, 60, 65, 65, 65, 70, 70).

**Row 1 (WS):** Starting in second ch from hook, 54 (59, 59, 64, 64, 64, 69, 69) sc. Turn.

**Row 2:** Ch 3, 1 dc, [skip 2 sc, (2 dc, ch 2, 2 dc) in next st, skip 2 sc] 10 (11, 11, 12, 12, 12, 13, 13) times, 2 dc. Turn. 44 (48, 48, 52, 52, 52, 56, 56) sts.

**Rows 3–4:** Ch 3, 1 dc, [skip 2 dc, (3 dc, ch 2, 3 dc) in ch2-space, skip 2 dc] 10 (11, 11, 12, 12, 12, 13, 13) times, 2 dc. Turn. 64 (70, 70, 76, 76, 76, 82, 82) sts.

**Row 5:** Ch 3, 1 dc, [skip 3 dc, (4 dc, ch 2, 4 dc) in ch2-space, skip 3 dc] 10 (11, 11, 12, 12, 12, 13, 13) times, 2 dc. Turn. 84 (92, 92, 100, 100, 100, 108, 108) sts.

### For sizes Newborn and Baby ONLY

**Row 6:** Ch3, 1 dc, [skip 4 dc, 8 dc in ch2-space, skip 4dc] 10 (11, -, -, -, -, -, -) times, 2 dc. Turn. 84 (92, -, -, -, -, -, -)sts.

### For 1-2y, 2y, 4y, 8y, 10y sizes ONLY

**Row 6:** Ch 3, [skip 4 dc, (4 dc, ch 2, 4 dc) in ch2-space, skip 4 dc] - (11, 11, 12, 12, 12, 13, 13) times, 2 dc. Turn.

**Row 7:** Ch 3, 1 dc, [skip 4 dc, (5 dc, ch 2, 5 dc) in ch2-space, skip 4 dc] - (-, 11, 12, 12, 12, 13, 13) times, 2 dc. Turn. - (-, 114, 124, 124, 124, 134, 134) sts.

**Row 8:** Ch 3, 1 dc, [skip 5 dc, (10dc) in ch2-

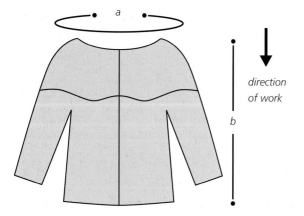

*a*

*direction of work*

*b*

space, skip 5 dc] - (-, 11, 12, 12, 12, 13, 13) times, 2 dc. Turn. - (-, 114, 124, 124, 124, 134, 134) sts.

## Body

### For ALL sizes

**Row 1:** With RS facing, join Color B. Working in BLO, ch 3, ldc in each stitch across, inc 2 (5, 0, 0, 0, 4, 0, 3) times evenly spaced across row. Turn. 86 (97, 114, 124, 124, 128, 134, 137) sts.
Work even in ldc for 1 (1, 0, 0, 2, 3, 4, 5) rows.

### Divide for Armholes

**Row 1:** Ch 3, 13 (14, 16, 17, 18, 20, 21, 22) ldc, 9 (9, 7, 9, 11, 12, 14, 15) ch, skip 14 (17, 21, 24, 22, 21, 22, 22) dc, 1 dc, 29 (32, 37, 39, 41, 43, 45, 47) ldc, 9 (9, 7, 9, 11, 12,

14, 15) ch, skip 14 (17, 21, 24, 22, 21, 22, 22) dc, 1 dc, 13 (14, 16, 17, 18, 20, 21, 22) ldc. Turn. 58 (63, 72, 76, 80, 86, 90, 93) sts. Work even in ldc (working into both chains and stitches for first row) for 10 (11, 12, 13, 13, 14, 18, 20) rows. 76 (81, 86, 94, 102, 110, 118, 123) sts. Break yarn.

### Sleeves (Make 2)

**Rnd 1:** Rejoin Color B at center of underarm sts, RS facing. Working into other side of ch and each st around, ch 3, 22 (25, 27, 32, 32, 32, 35, 36) ldc. Join into top of t-ch. Turn. 23 (26, 28, 33, 33, 33, 36, 37) sts.
Work even in ldc for 10 (12, 14, 17, 20, 23, 26, 27) rows. Break yarn.

### Button Band

**Row 1:** Rejoin Color A in bottom front hem,

RS facing. Make 2 sc into end of each row to collar. Turn. 38 (40, 44, 46, 50, 54, 64, 70) sts.
**Rows 2–3:** Ch 1, sc across. Turn.

### Buttonholes (work on right front facing side for girls)

**Row 1:** Rejoin Color A in bottom front hem, WS facing. Make 2 sc into end of each row to collar. Turn. 38 (40, 44, 46, 50, 54, 64, 70) sts.
**Row 2:** Ch 1, sc across. Turn.
**Row 3:** Ch 1, [3 sc, ch 1, skip 1 sc] 9 (9, 10, 11, 12, 13, 15, 17) times, 2 (4, 4, 2, 2, 2, 4, 2) sc. Break yarn. 29 (31, 34, 35, 38, 41, 49, 53) sts.

### Finishing

Using the buttonholes as a guide, sew on your buttons.

# Sources for Supplies

To find a local source for the yarns used in this book, contact the manufacturers below.

Cascade Yarns
http://www.cascadeyarns.com

Coats and Crafts
http://www.makeitcoats.com/en-us/explore/store-finder

Millia Mia / Classic Elite Yarns
http://www.classiceliteyarns.com/home.php

Rowan Yarns / Westminster Fibers
http://www.westminsterfibers.com/

Knitting Fever / Debbie Bliss yarn
http://knittingfever.com/brand/debbie-bliss/

Erika Knight Yarns
http://bluewaterfibers.com/

Artesano Ltd
Makers of alpaca and merino wools.
http://www.artesanoyarns.co.uk/

Magpielly Yarns
Selling Brown Sheep Yarns.
http://www.magpielly.co.uk

Designer Yarns
Providers of Debbie Bliss wools.
http://www.designeryarns.uk.com/

Eden Cottage Yarns
Hand-dyed wool from Yorkshire.
http://www.edencottageyarns.co.uk/

Erika Knight Wools
British wools in gorgeous muted pallets.
http://www.erikaknight.co.uk/

Fireside Yarn
Supplier of recycled cotton jersey yarn.
http://www.firesideyarn.co.uk/

Fyberspates
Hand-dyed yarn in a range of weights and fibers.
http://www.fyberspates.co.uk/

Jamieson's
Suppliers of Shetland wool.
http://www.jamiesonsofshetland.co.uk/

Libby Summers Ltd
Purveyor of Peruvian wool and alpaca yarns.
http://www.libbysummers.co.uk/

Malabrigo Yarns
Providers of a range of wool in beautiful hand-dyed colors.
http://www.malabrigoyarn.com/

Nutscene 1922
Makers of garden twine.
http://www.nutscene.com/

Quince and Co.
Gorgeous yarns in a range of subtle colors and variety of weights.
http://quinceandco.com/

Ripples Craft
Beautiful hand-dyed yarn, inspired by the landscape of Assynt.
https://www.ripplescrafts.com/

Rico Design
A range of beautiful and affordable cotton and wool yarns.
http://www.rico-design.de/

Sublime Yarns/Sirdar Spinning Ltd
Manufacturers of Sublime and Sirdar yarns.
http://www.sirdar.co.uk/home

## Other Craft Supplies
**Yarns, Hooks and Other Notions**

UK
Loop Knitting
http://www.loopknittingshop.com

McA Direct
http://www.mcadirect.com

Australia
Morris and Sons
http://morrisandsons.com.au/

The Wool Shack
http://www.thewoolshack.com/

New Zealand
Knit World
http://www.knitting.co.nz/

The Yarn Studio
http://www.theyarnstudio.co.nz/

# Index

# Acknowledgments

To my truly amazing friend, tech editor, support and partner in all things crochet, Joanne Scrace—thank you doesn't really cover how much I appreciate everything you do.

Thanks to the truly dream team of Vicky Orchard (editor), Nadine Tubbs (stylist) and Louise Leffler (designer) for bringing my work to life with such artistry. Kyle Books makes the most beautiful books and I am honored to have mine amongst them. Thank you as well to Abbi Rose Crook for her make-up artistry, our collection of models—Sinead, Chelsea, Steve, Alberto, Lara, Iris and Greta, and to Boden for supplying their wardrobes. Thanks as always to Clare Hulton, agent extraordinaire, for all her hard work behind the scenes. Thank you to my sample makers—Joanne, Rita, Jacqui, Elly and Jessica. I couldn't have done it without you!

Thanks to my long-suffering business partner, Kat Molesworth, for unending advice and for taking the reins when I have to hide away to write books.

Thank you to my friends and family: Julia, Kerstin, David and Ingrid for jumping in to help whenever and wherever it's needed as we try to juggle book and house, business and life—even if it's just a bottle of wine or a slice of cake at exactly the right moment.

And finally, thank you to Kevin, Ellis, Theo and Georgia—I love you more than anything.